PLAYBACK+
Speed • Pitch • Balance • Loop

Transcriptions • Lessons • Bios • Photos

25 GREAT CL[...] SOLOS

eaturing Pop, Rock, Jazz, Blues, and Classical Clarinet Legends, including Buddy DeFranco, Benny oodman, Ross Gorman, Pee Wee Russell, Artie Shaw, Jan Van Halen, Phil Woods and Many More

by Eric J. Morones

To access audio, visit:
www.halleonard.com/mylibrary

Enter Code
1880-9382-0292-8060

Cover Photo Credits:
Artie Shaw Photo by Michael Ochs Archives/Getty Images
Buddy DeFranco Photo courtesy William P. Gottlieb/Ira and Leonore S. Gershwin Fund Collection, Music Division, Library of Congress.
Johnny Dodds Photo by Gilles Petard/Redferns
Pee Wee Russell Photo courtesy William P. Gottlieb/Ira and Leonore S. Gershwin Fund Collection, Music Division, Library of Congress.
Benny Goodman Photo courtesy William P. Gottlieb/Ira and Leonore S. Gershwin Fund Collection, Music Division, Library of Congress.
Acker Bilk Photo by David Farrell/Redferns

ISBN 978-1-5400-6632-9

Visit Hal Leonard Online at
www.halleonard.com

World headquarters, contact:
Hal Leonard
7777 West Bluemound Road
Milwaukee, WI 53213
Email: info@halleonard.com

In Europe, contact:
Hal Leonard Europe Limited
1 Red Place
London, W1K 6PL
Email: info@halleonardeurope.com

In Australia, contact:
Hal Leonard Australia Pty. Ltd.
4 Lentara Court
Cheltenham, Victoria, 3192 Australia
Email: info@halleonard.com.au

Preface

25 Great Clarinet Solos is a collection of some of the most renowned and significant clarinet solos and melodies ever recorded. The songs themselves are classics: famous, recognizable, and heard almost everywhere in the world. For the person who has always wanted to learn those famous clarinet melodies ("licks"), it's all here!

Solos/songs were chosen using various criteria: popularity, acquirable publishing rights, musical content, familiarity, and inherent musicality. Some are harder than others, and some are short and simple. Extensive research was done to provide accurate information about the solos, songs, equipment used, recording, musicians, and players. (In some instances, that info was simply unavailable.)

A few solos are performed on bass clarinet. Since bass clarinet sounds an octave lower, playing the parts an octave lower on the B♭ clarinet will match the correct pitch. Certain solos contain some precarious high notes, so study proper high-note fingerings (included at the end of the book) and practice appropriate high-note exercises.

About the Audio

The accompanying audio tracks attempt to sound like the original recordings. The time code shown at the start of each solo transcription indicates the point where the solo begins on the original recording. There are two versions of each solo: 1) clarinet solo with accompaniment; 2) accompaniment only. This allows you to hear how the solo sounds, then to play it yourself with the accompaniment track. Though our goal was to replicate all solos and performances, there's nothing like the real thing, so we encourage you to listen to the original recordings.

All music on the recordings is performed by:

Eric J. Morones	clarinet, bass clarinet, saxophones, keyboards
Austin Byrd	piano
Lucky Diaz	guitar
Anders Swanson	bass
Brennan Murray	drums
Nathan Morones	trumpet

Orchestral arrangement of *Rhapsody in Blue* by Kyle Newmaster
Produced by Eric J. Morones
Recorded and Mixed by Nic Chaffee at Woodshed Studios, Long Beach, California

Thank you to Jeff Schroedl and Hal Leonard LLC, to the wonderful musicians on this project, and to all the amazing clarinetists who played these great solos that will last a lifetime!

Contents

PAGE	SONG	CLARINET PLAYER
4	Canal Street Blues	Johnny Dodds
6	Rhapsody in Blue	Ross Gorman
8	The Mooch	Barney Bigard
11	Sugar Foot Stomp	Russell Procope
13	Bugle Call Rag	Pee Wee Russell
15	Sing, Sing, Sing	Benny Goodman
19	Nightmare	Artie Shaw
21	Stealin' Apples	Benny Goodman
23	High Society	Alphonse Picou
25	Stardust	Artie Shaw
27	A Foggy Day (In London Town)	Buddy DeFranco
30	Stranger on the Shore	Acker Bilk
32	When I'm Sixty-Four	Robert Burns, Henry MacKenzie, Frank Reidy
37	Shake 'Em Up	Henry Diltz
39	Better Days	Sermon Posthumas
41	Nineteen Hundred and Eighty-Five	Unknown
43	Scenes from an Italian Restaurant	Richie Cannata
45	Sabu Visits the Twin Cities Alone	Jim Rothermel
47	Take the Long Way Home	John Helliwell
49	Breakfast in America	John Helliwell
51	Here's Looking at You	Unknown
53	Big Bad Bill (Is Sweet William Now)	Jan Van Halen
56	Nostalgia	Phil Woods
60	On Your Shore	Neil Buckley
62	Come	Kathy Jensen

Johnny Dodds

"It was my ambition to play as he did. I still think that if it had not been for Joe 'King' Oliver, jazz would not be what it is today."
–Louis Armstrong

Johnny Dodds

The first solo of the bunch is proof that great performances will last a century!

Johnny Dodds was born on April 12, 1892 in Waveland, Mississippi. He received his first clarinet around age 16, with early jazz pioneer Sidney Bechet as his first influence. Dodds eventually moved to New Orleans where he practiced during his job lunch breaks. Like many New Orleans musicians at the time, he sharpened his music reading and playing skills working in dance bands aboard Mississippi riverboats. In 1920, he relocated to Chicago, where he replaced Jimmie Noone in the powerful and popular King Oliver's Creole Jazz Band. A young Louis Armstrong, who was also in Oliver's band, later invited Dodds to play an important role in his first recordings—as a leader with legendary Hot Seven. "Canal Street Blues" and "Potato Head Blues" are just a few examples of famous performances from the band.

In total, Dodds eventually played on nearly 220 recordings with various bands and orchestras, including Kid Ory's Creole Orchestra, Papa Celestin's Original Tuxedo Band, Jelly Roll Morton's Red Hot Peppers, and his ow Johnny Dodds and his Chicago Boy Orchestra. His unique clarinet to was known for its wide vibrato, stro attacks, deep blues inflections and roo and flowing diatonic melodies.

Dodds died of a heart attack on August 1940 in Chicago.

King Oliver

King Oliv

Joseph Nathan "King" Oliver was born December 19, 1881 in Aben, Louisian As a trumpet player and bandlead he was one of the most important ear figures in jazz. Oliver began playi cornet as a child in a neighborho brass band. He would later become t teacher of the young Louis Armstron As a bandleader and composer, wrote many classic popular jazz hi cluding "Dippermouth Blues," "Sweet ke This," "Doctor Jazz," and "Canal reet Blues." Oliver became famous r using mutes, derbies, bottles, and ps to alter the sound of his cornet. By 22, he was considered the "King of zz," leading the legendary King Oliver d His Creole Jazz Band.

iver died in Savannah, Georgia on oril 10, 1938.

How to Play It

'anal Street Blues" is credited to both liver and Lil Hardin Armstrong, Louis Armstrong's second wife. It was the second title from King Oliver's Creole Jazz Band's first recording session, held on April 5, 1923 in Richmond, Indiana.

To play it, you will have to use note bends or scoops, performed by dropping your jaw to lower the pitch, and then back up while still maintaining the note. A wide and shaky vibrato (a style of the 1920s) is played on all long, sustained notes. Play with an open "oh" embouchure to give you a wider, open-sounding Dodds tone! Dodds used a Selmer Albert-System clarinet, which allowed greater flexibility in his sound and made it easier to bend notes and create smears. Some higher notes, including the high-range G, are required in measures 13-14. Use straight-eighth notes rather than the usual swing-eighth notes.

Vital Stats

Clarinet player: Johnny Dodds

Song: "Canal Street Blues"

Album: *King Oliver's Creole Jazz Band*

Age at time of recording: 41

Clarinet used: Selmer Albert-System

Mouthpiece: unknown

Words and Music by Joe Oliver

Ross Gorman

Photo courtesy Library of Congress, Prints & Photographs Division

Ross Gorman

This composition puts the "classic" in classical! One of 20th-century music's most famous pieces just happens to feature a famous clarinet intro—that was made purely by accident!

Ross Gorman was born on November 18, 1890 in Patterson, New Jersey. He studied music with his musician father, John R. Gorman, appearing with him as part of the vaudeville act The Kiltie Trio. In 1919, Gorman joined Harry Yerkes' Band, recording several albums with Columbia Records. Forming his own band, Novelty Syncopators, they recorded many novelty songs, the most famous of which was "Barkin' Dog Blues;" it featured the clarinet imitating a barking dog.

The well-known band leader Paul Whiteman hired Gorman for his orchestra in late October 1920, where he replaced Gus Mueller; he stayed with the band for five years. It was during this period that he was featured in the premiere performance of George Gershwin's *Rhapsody in Blue* (February 12, 1924). He eventually formed his own orchestra, appearing in *The Earl Carroll's Vanities 1925 Revue.* Throughout the 1930s, he performed a lot of radio and studio work and was a staff musician for NBC, recording with many bands, including the boy-wonder trumpet player B. A. Rolfe.

Ross Gorman died on February 27, 1953.

George Gershwin

Jacob Bruskin Gershowitz (Georg Gershwin) was born on September 26 1898 in Brooklyn, New York. Whe the family bought an upright piano i 1910, he quickly learned to play it; b age 15, he was writing his own songs His first published song came out a age 17. He and his wordsmith brothe Ira wrote several successful musicals including the hits *Oh, Lady Be Good Funny Face*, and *Strike Up the Band* Gershwin's many contributions to th Great American Songbook includ "Fascinating Rhythm," "I Got Rhythm," "Summertime," and "A Foggy Day" (see page 27). Among his other composition are the opera *Porgy and Bess*, the orchestral tone poem *An American in Paris* and, of course, *Rhapsody in Blue*.

Gershwin died of a brain tumor on Jul 11, 1937 in Hollywood, California.

How to Play It

In 1924, Paul Whiteman (1890-1967) the country's best-known band leade from the 1920s to the 1940s, tappe Gershwin to write a "jazz concerto for a concert he planned to present a New York's Aeolian Hall. (Whitema had been impressed by his earlie collaboration with Gershwin on *Georg White's Scandals of 1922.*) Entitled "A Experiment in Modern Music," it prom ised to broaden concertgoers' percep tions of what serious American musi could sound like.

George Gershwin

"It was on the train, with its steely rhythms, its rattle-ty bang, that is so often so stimulating to a composer. I frequently hear music in the very heart of the noise. And there I suddenly heard, and even saw on paper, the complete construction of the Rhapsody, *from beginning to end."*

–George Gershwin on *Rhapsody in Blue*

he famous opening clarinet solo ıme during a rehearsal when, as a ıke, Gorman played the notes with a oticeable, over-exaggerated glissando. ershwin liked it so much that he asked m to perform the opening measures ıat way at the concert and to add "as ıuch wail as possible." Originally, it as written as a simple scale run up to ıe top C.

o play this famous glissando effect, ide your fingers through the fingered otes, while slowing dropping your nbouchure. Merge the pitches until it's a slurred, bent effect between all the notes from low G to high C.

Measure 2 has a turn that can use the side C trill fingering to play between the B♭ and C. In Measure 6, use the side trill fingering for B♭ between the A and B♭. Measure 10 has a high F. Make sure the triplets are clean and even. Play all articulations as notated, with a "classical" tone.

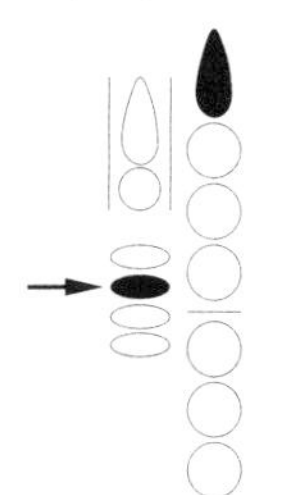

Vital Stats

Clarinet player: Ross Gorman

Song: *Rhapsody in Blue*

Album: Paul Whiteman and His Orchestra, *Rhapsody in Blue*, original 1924 acoustic 78 RPM

Age at time of recording: 34

Clarinet used: unknown

Mouthpiece: unknown

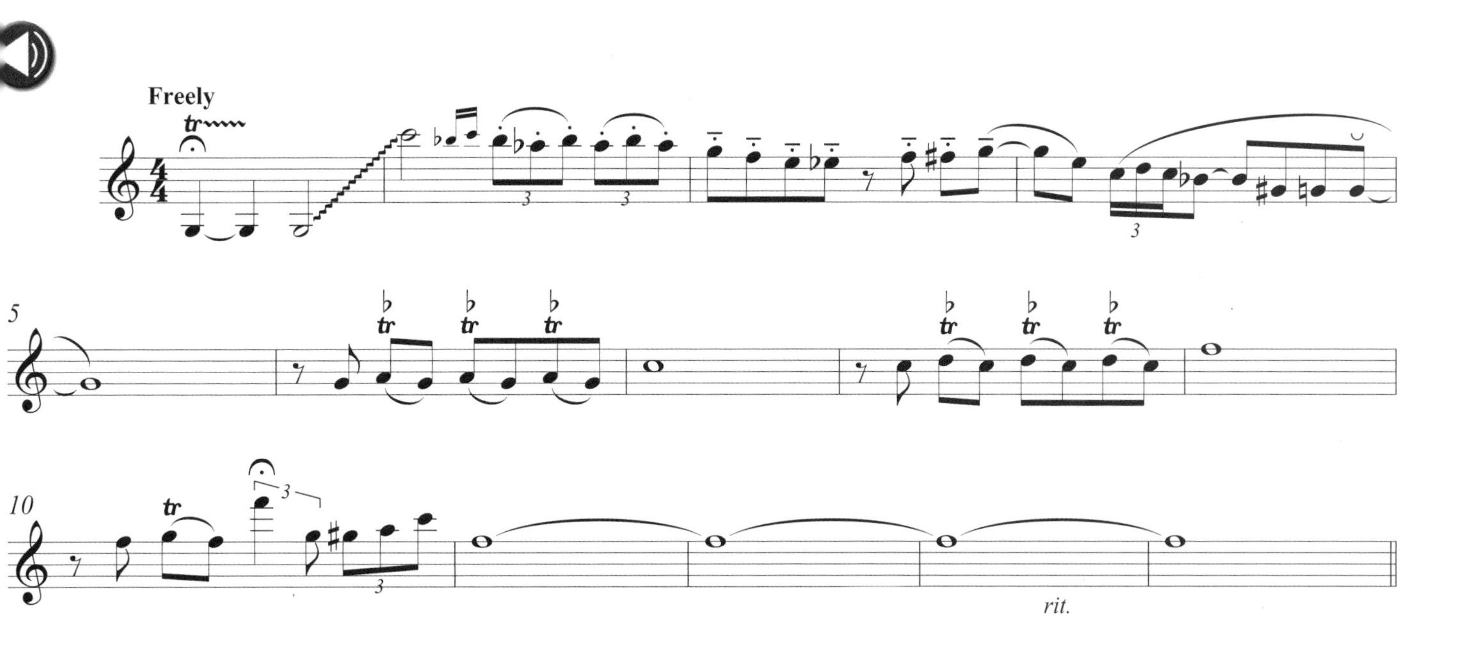

By George Gershwin

Barney Bigard

"The Mooch" features unusual blends of melodies and rhythms—as well as the unique instrumental colors of the players—all of which combine to make the special sound that was Duke Ellington.

Albany Leon "Barney" Bigard was born on March 3, 1906 in New Orleans. He took clarinet lessons with the famous Lorenzo Tio at an early age. In the early 1920s, he moved to Chicago, where he worked with King Oliver (see page 4) between 1925-27. Also known as a great tenor sax player, Bigard became known for his low-register, woody clarinet tone that people associate with New Orleans-style clarinetists. In 1927, Bigard joined Duke Ellington's Orchestra and played with them until 1942. With Ellington, he was a featured clarinet soloist and co-composed the jazz standard "Mood Indigo." Along with Ellington, he made famous recordings with trombonist Kid Ory, Louis Armstrong, Nat King Cole, Ella Fitzgerald, and groups under his own direction.

Photo courtesy William P. Gottlieb/Ira and Leonore S. Gershwin Fund Collection, Music Division, Library of Congress

Barney Bigard

After leaving Duke's band, Bigard moved to Los Angeles, where he did soundtrack work for many Hollywood film studios; he even had an onscreen featured role in *New Orleans* (1947). Throughout the 1960s, he led his own sextet, including tours of Europe and Africa for the State Department.

Bigard died on June 27, 1980, in Culver City, California. His autobiography, *With Louis and The Duke*, was released posthumously in 1988.

Duke Ellington

Duke Ellington

Edward Kennedy "Duke" Ellington wa born on April 29, 1899 in Washingto D.C. He began studying piano at ag seven, writing his first compositio "Soda Fountain Rag," at age 15.

He studied art during his high-scho years, almost choosing it as a caree Inspired by several ragtime performer at age 17 he began to perform profe sionally as a musician. During the 1920 Ellington formed his first sextets—ar soon, larger bands—that would becom the world-famous Duke Ellingto Orchestra. As a legendary pianist ar bandleader whose career spanned ov 50 years, he composed thousands scores, including famous songs lik "Sophisticated Lady," "Satin Doll, "Don't Get Around Much Any More "Prelude to a Kiss," "Solitude," "I Let Song Go Out of My Heart," and "Tak the 'A' Train" (co-written with Bil Strayhorn).

Ellington died of cancer on May 2 1974 in New York City.

‘There was something different about him. Everybody in the band knew they were working with a genius.”

Barney Bigard on Duke Ellington

How to Play It

Written by Ellington and Irving Mills in 1928, “The Mooche” comes from Ellington’s “jungle style,” African-themed music period, echoing other songs like “East St. Louis Toodle-oo” and “Black and Tan Fantasy.” The name, as Ellington explained, referred to “a certain lazy gait peculiar to some of the folk of Harlem.”

There are two solos here:

Solo 1 is the famous clarinet melody of the song, played in harmony with other clarinets. (The lead part is omitted for the backing track). Use a very wide vibrato and employ an open “oh” embouchure position, with an open throat.

Solo 2 is Bigard’s low-register “woody” solo. Try to overblow the clarinet, but avoid squawking or cracking any notes. Again, use lots of wide vibrato. Most of the lines are slurred, which should be helpful in playing.

Vital Stats

Clarinet player: Barney Bigard

Song: “The Mooche”

Album: unknown

Age at time of recording: 22

Clarinet used: Albert system

Mouthpiece: unknown

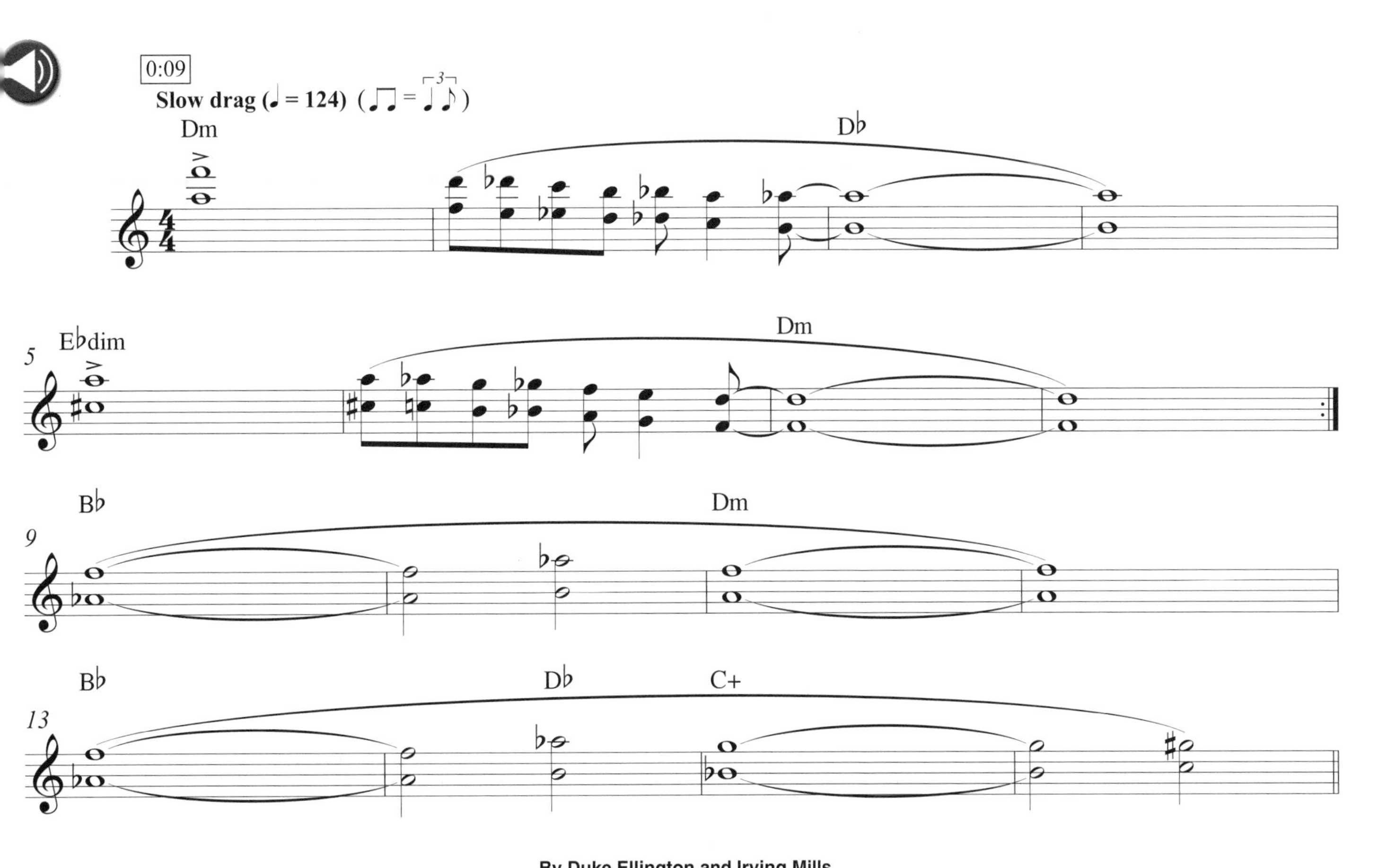

By Duke Ellington and Irving Mills

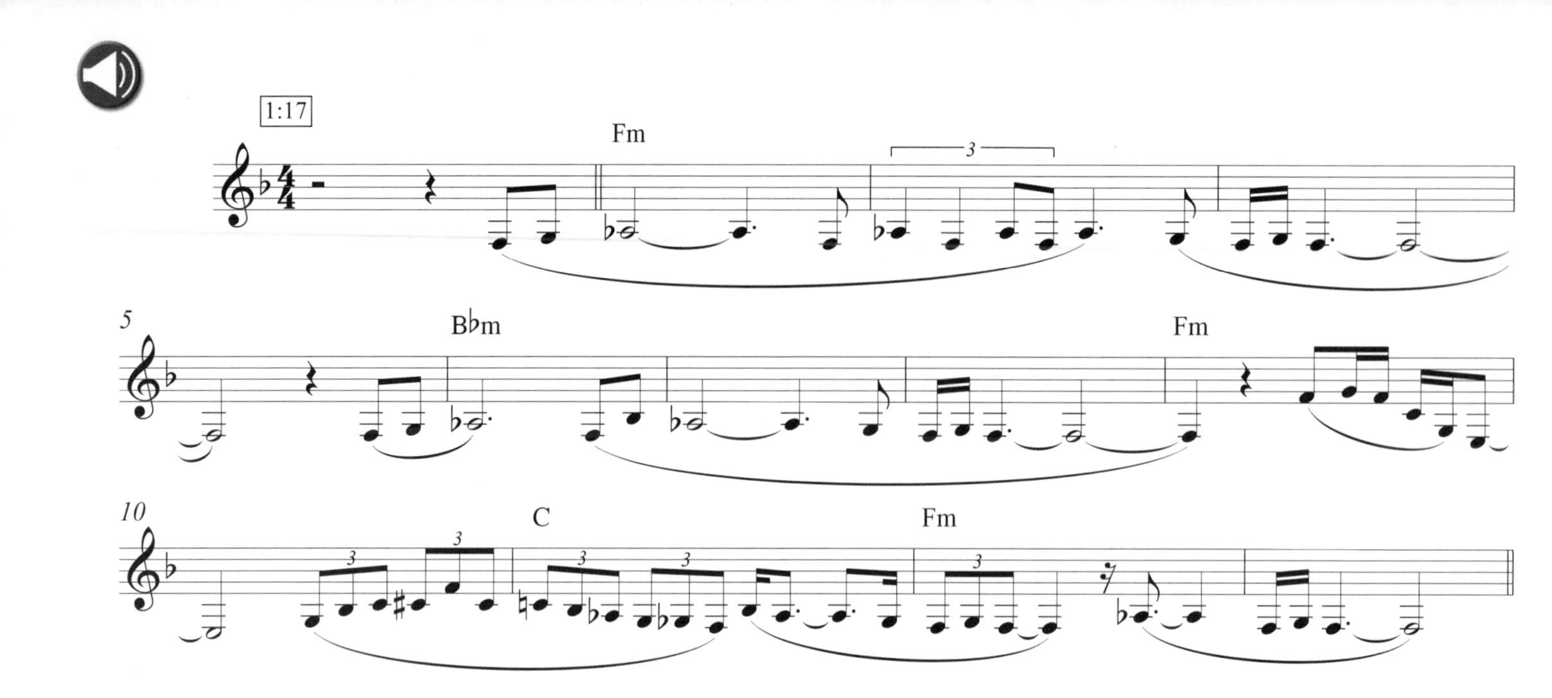
1:17
Fm
3
5
B♭m
Fm
10
3
3
3
3
C
Fm
3

Russell Procope

"I enjoyed every day I was a member of the Ellington band, even though it was grueling trying to keep up with Duke. But I knew I was a part of something that was very special, something that would never die."

-Russell Procope on Duke Ellington

Russell Procope

Fast fingers in the clarinet's chalumeau register (low notes) are required for this hair-raising solo!

Russell Procope was born on August 11, 1908 in New York City. His first instrument was the violin; he later switched to clarinet and alto saxophone. In 1926, Procope was a member of Billy Freeman's Orchestra and, at age 20, recorded with Jelly Roll Morton. He also played with bands led by Benny Carter, Chick Webb, Fletcher Henderson, McKinney's Cotton Pickers, Tiny Bradshaw, Teddy Hill, King Oliver, and Willie Bryant. From 1942 until the end of World War II, Procope served in the U.S. Army. After idolizing the Duke Ellington Orchestra for years, he was asked to play clarinet and alto saxophone with the band in 1945, taking over the chair held by Barney Bigard (see page 4). He made his reputation playing clarinet in this band, where Ellington wrote several pieces featuring him; these include "4:30 Blues," "Blues to Be There," "Second Line," and "Swamp Goo." Procope released his own recording, *The Persuasive Sax of Russ Procope*, in 1956 on the London record label. He continued with the Ellington band up until Ellington's death in 1974, becoming one of the ensemble's longstanding members. In the 1970s, he kept busy playing with Brooks Kerr's group.

Russell Procope died of a heart attack on January 21, 1981 in New York City.

Fletcher Henderson

Fletcher Henderson

James Fletcher Hamilton Henderson was born on December 18, 1897 in Cuthbert, Georgia. His mother taught him to play the piano, beginning lessons at age 6. By 13, Henderson could read music fluently and had developed a discerning ear. He attended Atlanta University as a chemistry and math major, graduating in 1920. While living in New York, he started work as a music director for many artists and projects.

In 1924, Henderson hired a young Louis Armstrong; the two made many influential jazz recordings together. He wrote many hit arrangements for Benny Goodman. In point of fact, his bands and arrangements defined the sound of big-band jazz in the 1920s and '30s. While accompanying Ethyl Waters on tour, Henderson fell ill and collapsed from a stroke. Forced to retire, he still remained one of the most influential arrangers and bandleaders in jazz history.

Henderson died on December 29, 1952 in New York City.

How to Play It

"Sugar Foot Stomp" is credited to Louis Armstrong and Don Redman. A 12-bar-blues form, Procope stays in the low register the whole time, so give that register key a rest! Blow hard, but avoid cracking any note. This one is technically challenging, so start slowly and use a metronome. (Beware of the leaps in measure 7.)

Vital Stats

Clarinet player: Russell Procope

Song: "Sugar Foot Stomp"

Album: *Fletcher Henderson*

Age at time of recording: 23

Clarinet used: Albert system

Mouthpiece: unknown

Lyric by Walter Melrose
Music by Joe Oliver

Pee Wee Russell

Photo courtesy William P. Gottlieb/Ira and Leonore S. Gershwin Fund Collection, Music Division, Library of Congress

Pee Wee Russell

"Pee Wee Russell had the most fabulous musical mind. I've never run into anybody who had that much musical talent."

–Gene Krupa, drummer and bandleader

"Bluesy" is the best word to describe this Pee Wee Russell solo!

Charles Ellsworth "Pee Wee" Russell was born on March 27, 1906 in St. Louis, Missouri. He began violin as a child, later playing piano and drums, before finally settling on the clarinet at age 13. Receiving the nickname "Pee Wee" because of his slight build, Russell began his career while still a teenager, playing in a Dixieland band. He became known for solos that contain growls, squeaks, and unpredictable note choices. In the mid-1920s, he was working with greats like Bix Beiderbecke, Frank Trumbauer, and Red Nichols and his Five Pennies. Russell moved to New York in the early '30s, where he would eventually perform with Billy Banks, Louis Prima, Bobby Hackett, Red Allen, Jack Bland, Buster Bailey, and Vic Dickenson and playing in modern settings with Thelonious Monk and Duke Ellington. He started working with Eddie Condon's groups, remaining with him off and on for 30 years.

Russell died on February 15, 1969 in Alexandria, Virginia.

Vital Stats

Clarinet player: Pee Wee Russell

Song: "Bugle Call Rag"

Album: *Billy Banks and His Orchestra*

Age at time of recording: 26

Clarinet used: Conn

Mouthpiece: unknown

How to Play It

"Bugle Call Rag" (also known as "Bugle Call Blues") is a jazz standard written by Jack Pettis, Billy Meyers, and Elmer Schoebel. First recorded in 1922, later renditions—as well as the published sheet music and the song's copyright—used the title "Bugle Call Rag." As a vintage jazz standard, it's been recorded by hundreds of players and featured in movies.

Although known for solos that contain left and right turns, Pee Wee's solo is somewhat tame, showing his bluesy side. Be sure to swing all the eighth notes while tonguing them; use a fat, wide vibrato. You'll need to be proficient on your side E♭ fingering!

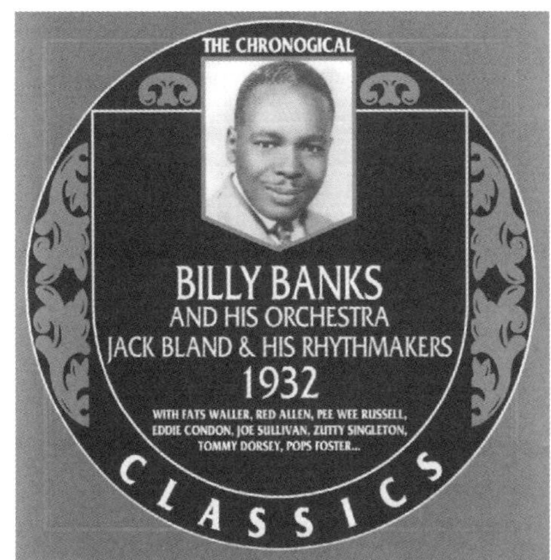

By Jack Pettis, Billy Meyers and Elmer Schoebel

Benny Goodman

'I was out at the race track ɒack in 1936 with Bing Crosby ɪnd George Raft. On the way ɪome, the phrase 'Sing, Bing, Sing' kept running through my nind. By the time I got home, ' decided that wasn't very :ommercial, and I changed it to Sing, Sing, Sing.'"

Louis Prima

Benny Goodman

'he King of Swing truly lives up to his ıoniker on this classic composition by .ouis Prima!

ɪenjamin David Goodman was born n May 30, 1909 in Chicago. At age 0, he delved into music at the Kehelah acob Synagogue. He studied the clarinet nder the tutelage of Chicago Symphony ıember Franz Schoepp. An obviously ifted, young player, Goodman began is professional career in his first pit and at age 11, becoming a member of ıe American Federation of Musicians t 14. He quit school and decided to ursue a career in music full time. When Benny was 16, he was hired by the Ben 'ollack Band and moved to Los Angeles, taying with the band for four years as ıeir featured soloist. In 1929, Goodman ɛft Pollack's group to participate in ecording sessions and radio shows in Jew York City, later working with jazz romoter John Hammond.

Iammond, who launched the recording areers of Billie Holiday and Count Basie, among many others, wanted Benny to record with drummer Gene Krupa and trombonist Jack Teagarden. Those recordings began to cement Benny's national popularity as the King of Swing. By 1934, Goodman led his own bands and began a residency at Billy Rose's Music Hall, playing Fletcher Henderson's arrangements—along with band members Bunny Berigan, Gene Krupa, and Jess Stacy. One of the greatest clarinetists of all time, he reached the height of his popularity in the 1930s, recording songs that would become Swing-era anthems. These include "Let's Dance," "Stomping at the Savoy," "King Porter Stomp," "Roll 'Em," and, of course, "Sing, Sing, Sing." Throughout his career, he remained a popular soloist and concert draw.

Goodman died of heart failure on June 13, 1986 in New York City.

Vital Stats

Clarinet player: Benny Goodman

Song: "Sing, Sing, Sing"

Album: unknown

Age at time of recording: 28

Clarinet used: Buffet Crampon R13

Mouthpiece: Selmer

Louis Prima

Louis Prima

Louis Leo Prima was born on December 7, 1910 in New Orleans. He started on violin, switching to cornet after borrowing one from his brother. He began gigging professionally at age 15. When Prima was 22, Guy Lombardo saw him perform and encouraged him to come to New York. There, he formed his own band, Louis Prima and his New Orleans Gang. From the 1940s through the 1960s, his musical vision expanded, encompassing early R&B, rock 'n' roll, and boogie-woogie. Prima also blended folk elements of his Italian and Sicilian heritage with jazz and swing music. He wrote many hit songs that are still covered today, including "Just a Gigolo," "Angelina," "Jump, Jive an' Wail," "Oh, Babe," and of course "Sing, Sing, Sing." In the '50s, he performed frequently as a Vegas lounge act, beginning with saxophonist Sam Butara and his then-wife, singer Keely Smith. He was featured in the 1967 Disney movie *The Jungle Book*—as King Louie the Orangutan—singing "I Wan'na Be Like You." Capitol Records signed Prima, releasing seven albums, including *The Wildest*.

Prima died on August 24, 1978 in New Orleans, Louisiana.

How to Play It

"Sing, Sing, Sing" was written by Prima in 1936. It was first recorded with the New Orleans Gang. The song is strongly identified with the big-band and Swing eras, thanks to instrumental performances by Fletcher Henderson and, most famously, Benny Goodman. Goodman's version was inducted into the Grammy Hall of Fame in 1982, and continues to be heard in many films and television shows.

With drummer Gene Krupa as the backing track, Goodman's open solo features great lines all over the clarinet. You'll want to swing all eight notes, and tongue each one. Measures 28-29 have high D that needs some vibrato. Measure 37-39 are technically difficult, so prac tice slowly first—especially measure 3 with its C♯ (right or left)—until you'r comfortable with it. Measures 45-5 have some difficult interval leaps. Kee your embouchure still when playing moving your jaw or embouchure wi make those notes crack. Measure 52 ha an arpeggio that lands on a high F♯ tha moves to a high G in measure 53; mak the transition between those two pitche clean and solid, and don't move you embouchure. Moving from measure 5 to 56, glissando as many notes possibl between the high A and the downbeat B♭ but keep it clean. Measures 56-57 hav a pleasing diminished arpeggio that i not often played in a solo. In measure 74-79, pay attention to the notated trill and when to stop them.

Words and Music by Louis Prima

42
46
50
54
58
62
66
70
74
78

Artie Shaw

Photo courtesy William P. Gottlieb/Ira and Leonore S. Gershwin Fund Collection, Music Division, Library of Congress

Artie Shaw

haw's "Nightmare" is a masterpiece—nd one of the hardest solos your author as ever played!

rthur Jacob Arshawsky (Artie Shaw) as born on May 23, 1910 in New ork City. He played the ukulele at age 0, alto saxophone at age 12, finally witching to clarinet at 16. He formed his first band, called the Bellevue Ramblers, while still in his teens. From 1926 to 1929, he lived and worked in Cleveland as a music director and arranger for an orchestra led by violinist Austin Wylie, quickly becoming a successful session musician. He made his first public appearance as a leader in 1936, the first white front man to hire a full-time black female singer (Billie Holiday) to tour the segregated South. In the 1930s and '40s, he pulled down a five-figure weekly salary and—along with Benny Goodman, Tommy Dorsey, and Glenn Miller—helped make Swing music popular.

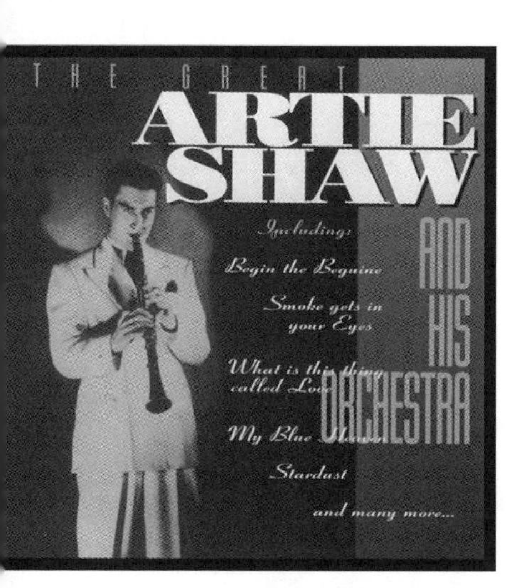

As a solo artist, Shaw became best known for his 1938 recording of Cole Porter's "Begin the Beguine;" other popular hits include "Stardust" (see page 25), "Back Bay Shuffle," "Moonglow," "Nightmare," "Rosalie," and "Frenesi," as well as his "Concerto for Clarinet" (1940). Shaw hated the loss of privacy that stardom brought, and retired from jazz almost totally after 1954, laying the clarinet aside until 1983. He wrote three short novels, including his autobiographical book *The Trouble with Cinderella*, released in 1952.

Shaw died of natural causes on December 30, 2004 in Thousand Oaks, California.

How to Play It

"Nightmare" was composed by Shaw in 1936 and was first released on *Artie Shaw and His Orchestra* in 1938. It became the opening theme of his orchestra's live radio broadcasts and the band's signature song. Sounding dark and scary, some say it may have inspired John Barry to write his famous "James Bond Theme."

This solo is difficult, featuring a flurry of masterful lines. Practice slowly at first.

The opening phrase is challenging, playing the F♯ to B over the break. Measure 7 is a tough line, too. Here, focus on hitting the target downbeat Bs. All long, sustained notes have vibrato on them. Measures 11-17 feature some serious high-note passages. Practice the finger transitions slowly and make sure your high notes are strong and maintained. (See fingering chart at the end of the book.) Measure 15 has a high B, so you'll need a strong reed. In measure 17, simply do a glissando (whatever notes you want) and land on the downbeat low F♯. The low F♯ is the important, target note in Measure 18. Just when you thought the hard part was over, measures 21-22 have a fast, diatonic pattern based on the B harmonic minor scale.

Vital Stats

Clarinet player: Artie Shaw

Song: "Nightmare"

Album: *Artie Shaw and His Orchestra,* 78 RPM

Age at time of recording: 26

Clarinet used: Conn

Mouthpiece: unknown

"That's the clarinet I used to use...but it's just a piece of wood, you know, with holes in it and they put these clumsy keys on it and you're supposed to try to take that and manipulate it with throat muscles and chops...and try to make something happen that never happened before. And when you do, you never forget it. It beats sex, it beats anything."

–Artie Shaw

By Artie Shaw

3enny Goodman

"You have to have courage and confidence in your own ability. You have to know what the hell and who the hell you are in this business. Music may change, but I don't think that ever will."

–Benny Goodman

Photo courtesy Library of Congress Prints and Photographs Division. New York World-Telegram and the Sun Newspaper Photograph Collection.

Fats Waller

ere's another masterful solo from the King of Swing! ee Benny Goodman's bio on page 15.

ats Waller

homas Wright "Fats" Waller was born n May 21, 1904 in New York City. His ther was a pastor and musician. Fats arted playing the piano at age six. By ge 15, he was a professional organist, nd was making records by the time he as 18. The founder of stride piano, he opyrighted over 400 songs, including Squeeze Me," "Ain't Misbehavin'," Black and Blue," and "Honeysuckle ose;" he also wrote for numerous usicals. In 1934, he formed his own roup, Fats Waller and His Rhythm, and recorded many records for RCA Victor. Waller was one of the most popular performers of his era, touring internationally and achieving critical and commercial success around the world as a supreme entertainer. He also appeared in two films, *King of Burlesque* (1936) and *Stormy Weather* (1943).

Waller died from pneumonia on December 15, 1943 in Kansas City, Missouri.

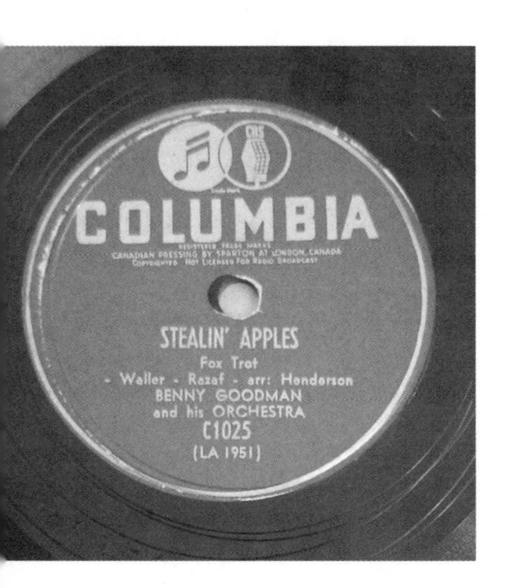

How to Play It

"Stealin' Apples" was written by Waller and was first recorded by Fletcher Henderson and His Orchestra in 1936. Benny Goodman recorded many versions of this song. In his 1939 rendition, Goodman stays in the high range throughout the solo. Measure 10 features a high B, which may be hard for some. Use vibrato on all high notes. In measure 12, hit that bluesy G with a note scoop. The turns in measures 17-18 should be practiced slowly, especially since it is not a commonly played pattern. Measure 24 has another high B, and measure 26 has another bluesy lowered 3rd (G). In measures 31-32, drop your jaw downward to bend the notes lower.

Vital Stats

Clarinet player: Benny Goodman

Song: "Stealin' Apples"

Album: *Benny Goodman and His Orchestra*

Age at time of recording: 30

Clarinet used: Buffet R13

Mouthpiece: unknown

Words by Andy Razaf
Music by Thomas "Fats" Waller

Alphonse Picou

lphonse Picou was a legend, one of he early pioneers of New Orleans jazz larinet.

lphonse Floristan Picou was born on)ctober 19, 1878 in New Orleans. He ook up guitar, but switched to clarnet when inspired by performances at he French Opera House there. Playing rofessionally at age 16, Picou was a nember a myriad of brass bands and lance bands that later helped develop vhat became "jazz." In his early 20s, icou traveled to Texas and Oklahoma vith a carnival show that included amous ensembles such as the Excelsior Brass Band, Freddie Keppard's Olympia)rchestra, and the Tuxedo Brass Band. Around 1915, he played briefly in Chicago with Manuel Perez, but soon fterward returned to New Orleans. In 932, he left the music business and vorked as a tinsmith. Picou returned to is earlier calling in the 1940s, making ecords with Papa Celestin and Kid Rena, as well as leading his own small group in New Orleans. His genius solo n "High Society" made him famous; t soon became a test piece for all New)rleans clarinetists.

Jazz musicians Papa Celestin (left) and Alphonse Picou, New Orleans, 1950

Picou died on February 4, 1961 in New Orleans, Louisiana.

How to Play It

Composer Porter Steele penned "High Society" as a march in 1901. It was never intended to be a jazz song, and the original sheet music had no solos in it. However, its popular band arrangement had a piccolo obbligato in it. Picou adapted that piccolo solo into a personalized clarinet solo; soon, everyone copied it and it became famous.

Clarinetists commonly solo through Picou's version (or one closely related), then do their own improvisational solo. Saxophonist Charlie "Bird" Parker famously quotes Picou's solo melody on his 1945 recording of "Ko Ko."

Be sure to play all eighth notes with a straight-eighth feel, not swing. The solo's phrasing has a march-like quality throughout; there's even a classical etude sound to it. Make note of all the specific articulations (slurs and tonguing). In measure 27, add a big scoop on the high C by dropping that jaw.

Vital Stats

Clarinet player: Alphonse Picou

Song: "High Society"

Album: *Kid Rena Band*

Age at time of recording: 61

Clarinet used: Albert system clarinet

Mouthpiece: unknown

"How did I happen to play 'High Society,' the famous chorus? Well, I was 17 at the time. I was playing with the Manuel Perez band, and he used to get all that old-time music. He bought that 'High Society' for me. It was a march tune. I took the piccolo part and transposed it to my instrument. It made a wonderful hit."

–Alphonse Picou

By Porter Steele and Walter Melrose

Artie Shaw

Let's learn another Shaw gem, this time on what some call "the song of the century"!

See Artie Shaw bio on page 19.

Hoagy Carmichael

Hoagland Howard "Hoagy" Carmichael was born on November 22, 1899 in Bloomington, Indiana. His mother taught him to sing and play the piano at an early age. He attended Indiana University studying law, but was busy as an accomplished jazz pianist. In 1922, he met cornetist Bix Beiderbecke, who hired him for his band, the Wolverines. Their performances inspired Carmichael's first composition, "Riverboat Shuffle." Other famous compositions include "Stardust," "Georgia on My Mind" (lyrics by Stuart Gorrell), "The Nearness of You," "Heart and Soul," and "Skylark," in collaboration with lyricist Johnny Mercer.

Carmichael won the 1951 Academy Award for Best Original Song for "In the Cool, Cool, Cool of the Evening." He also appeared as a character actor and musical performer in 14 films, hosted three musical-variety radio programs, performed on television, and wrote two autobiographies. *The Hoagy Carmichael Show* first went on the air at 5:30 pm Pacific Standard Time, on Sunday, October 26, 1946.

"And then it happened. That queer sensation that this melody was bigger than me. Maybe I hadn't written it at all. The recollection of how, when, and where it all happened became vague as the lingering strains hung in the rafters of the studio. I wanted to shout back at it, 'Maybe I didn't write you, but I found you.'"

–Hoagy Carmichael on "Stardust"

Hoagy Carmichael

How to Play It

Carmichael wrote "Stardust" in 1927, first recorded by Emil Seidel and His Orchestra and the Dorsey Brothers as a peppy but mid-tempo jazz instrumental. Mitchell Parish added lyrics and Carmichael reworked the song as a slow ballad. The bandleader/saxophonist Isham Jones recorded this new arrangement, which became the first of many hit records of the tune. The song became a Big Band standard, with just about every prominent bandleader and singer of the 1930s and '40s performing it, making "Stardust" one of the most recorded songs of the 20th century—almost 2,000 times.

Shaw's version has become a clarinet staple, a solo that is worth the effort to master. You can hear the melody through all his embellishments and turns; that's the beauty of it. Observe the notated articulations. Play all lines straight, not swung; use vibrato. Measures 13-14 are a beast of a line; make sure you have a strong reed and feel comfortable with the high-note fingerings.

Vital Stats

Clarinet player: Artie Shaw

Song: "Stardust"

Album: *Artie Shaw and His Orchestra* RCA Victor 45 RPM

Age at time of recording: 30

Clarinet Used: Conn

Mouthpiece: unknown

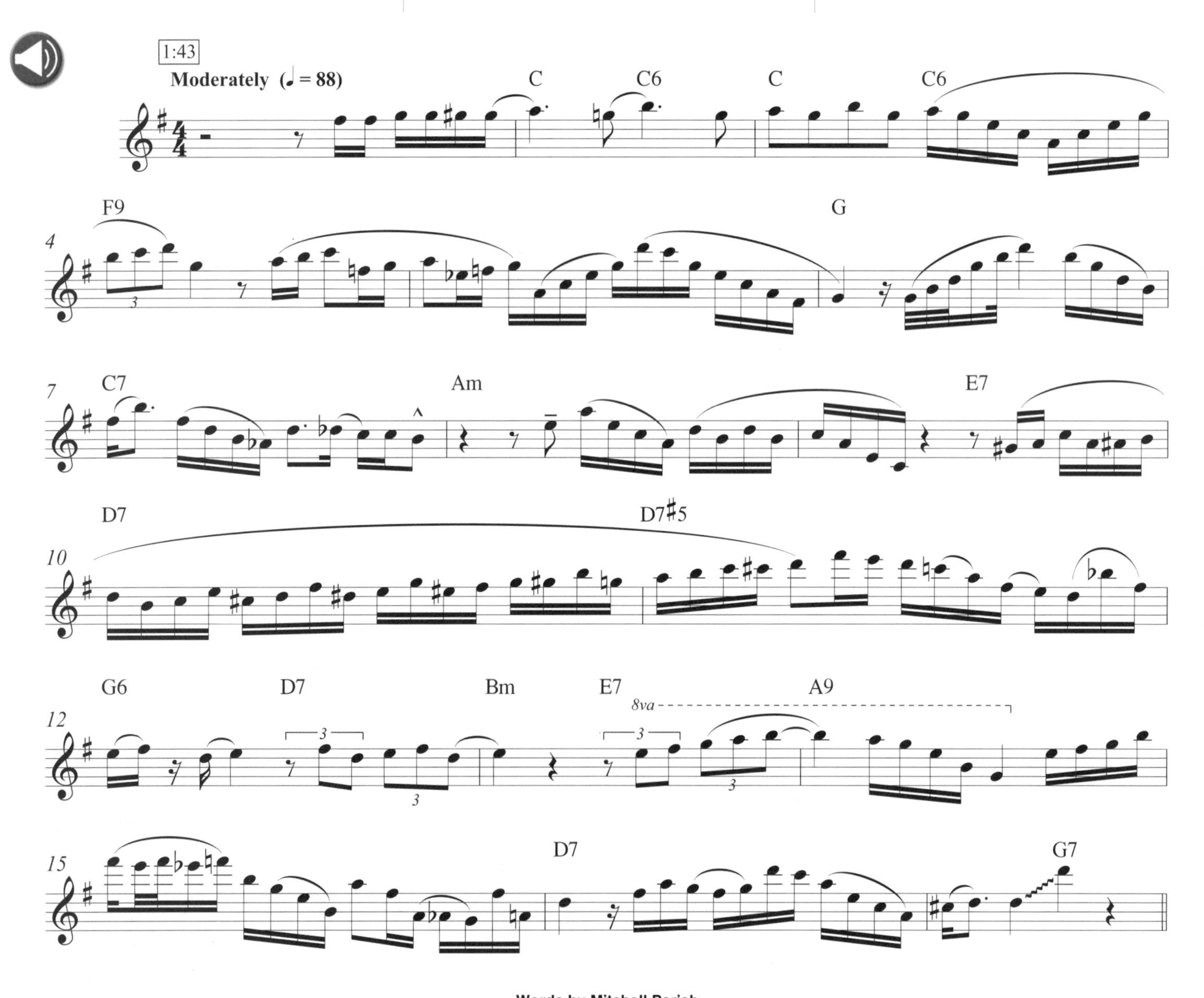

Words by Mitchell Parish
Music by Hoagy Carmichael

Buddy Defranco

Photo courtesy William P. Gottlieb/Ira and Leonore S. Gershwin Fund Collection, Music Division, Library of Congress.

Buddy DeFranco

"I guess I realized early on that to be a Benny Goodman or Artie Shaw clone wasn't going to mean very much. It's nice to attempt to play that well, but what's the point?"
–Buddy DeFranco

A Foggy Day (In London Town)" eatures a swingin', straight-ahead, ebop jazz solo by the great Buddy)efranco.

3oniface Ferdinand Leonard "Buddy")eFranco was born February 17, 1923 1 Camden, New Jersey. His father /as a talented musician and a piano tuner. Buddy began playing the clarinet around age nine. After attending the Mastbaum School of Music in Philadelphia, where he received classical training, he won a national Tommy Dorsey Talent Contest, which launched his career. In 1944, Tommy Dorsey hired DeFranco, who then spent four years with the most popular dance band of the era. He also played with Charlie Barnet and Count Basie's septet, but was mostly a bandleader from then on.

In the early 1950s, with pianist Sonny Clark and guitarist Tal Farlow, he recorded for the MGM and Verve labels. From 1960 to 1964, DeFranco released four innovative quartet albums as co-leader, with accordionist Tommy Gumina. Under the name The World Famous Glenn Miller Orchestra, Directed By Buddy DeFranco, he led the Glenn Miller Orchestra from 1966 to 1974. He also performed with Gene Krupa, Art Blakey, Art Tatum, Oscar Peterson, Lennie Tristano, Dodo Marmarosa, Terry Gibbs, Charlie Parker, Dizzy Gillespie, Miles Davis, and Billie Holiday. Buddy recorded more than 160 albums, and won the DownBeat All Stars Award 20 times.

DeFranco died on December 24, 2014 in Panama City, Florida.

How to Play It

"A Foggy Day (In London Town)" was composed by George Gershwin (see page 6), with lyrics by his brother Ira Gershwin. Fred Astaire introduced the song in the 1937 film *A Damsel in Distress*.

DeFranco's solo is straight-up bebop jazz, taking two choruses on this standard. Make sure to tongue all the eighth notes while swinging, and lay back a little throughout the solo. There's nothing crazy in the high range; everything is pretty much in the middle register. Take a lesson from the great bebop vocabulary in this solo!

Vital Stats

Clarinet player: Buddy DeFranco

Song: "A Foggy Day (In London Town)"

Album: *In a Mellow Mood*

Age at time of recording: 29

Clarinet used: unknown

Mouthpiece: unknown

from A DAMSEL IN DISTRESS
Music and Lyrics by George Gershwin and Ira Gershwin

37
G
B♭7
Am7
D7
41
Gmaj7
B♭7
Am7
D7
45
Dm7
G7
Cmaj7
D7
49
G
B♭7
Bm7
E7
Am7
D7
53
G
B♭7
Am7
D7
57
G
B♭7
Am7
D7
61
Dm7
G7
Cmaj7
Cm7
F7
65
Bm7
C
Bm7
Am7
Bm7
E7
Am7
D7
69
G
Am7
D7
Gmaj7

Acker Bilk

"It's all right, but you do get fed up with it after 50 years."
–Acker Bilk on "Stranger on the Shore"

Thanks to the film *Mr. Holland's Opus* (1995), a whole new generation was introduced to this wonderful song!

Bernard Stanley "Acker" Bilk was born on January 28, 1929 in Pensford, Somerset (U.K.).

His nickname "Acker" means "friend" or "mate" in Somerset slang. He tried playing piano as a child, but gave it up for outdoor activities. Those adventures cost him two front teeth in a school fight and half a finger in a sledging accident; both incidents affected his later clarinet style, Bilk said. He worked at the W.D. & H.O. Wills Cigarette Factory, then did three years of National Service with the Royal Engineers. While in the Army, he picked up the clarinet after a friend gave him one for free.

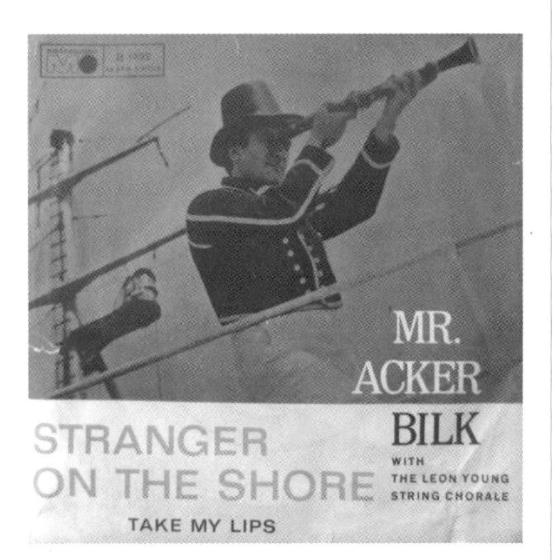

Bilk started earning his living on the "banjos-and-beer" circuit in the U.K., copying recordings of famous jazz musicians. He formed his first bands, Original Egyptian Stomper and Chew Valley Jazzmen. His hit song "Stranger on the Shore" was a No. 1 hit in 1962; other charting songs included "Above the Stars," "Summer Set," and "Buona Sera." Acker suffered several health scares during his later years, quickly recovering and performing. In 2001, he was awarded the M.B.E. (Member of the Order of the British Empire) in the Queen's New Years' Honours List for his services to jazz music.

Acker Bil

Bilk died on November 2, 2014.

How to Play It

Bilk's "Stranger on the Shore" was released in October 1961. Originally named "Jenny" for his daughter, he was asked to create the theme for a BBC-TV children's series about a French au pair in Brighton. Bilk offered them "Jenny," but was asked to change its title to the name of the program, *Stranger on the Shore*. Bilk claimed he thought up the song's melody in a taxi. The song become the U.K.'s biggest selling single of 1962, spending 55 weeks on the charts, and peaking at No. 2; it also became the No. 1 single in the United States on the Billboard Hot 100 Pop chart. As an instrumental, it was covered by Booke T. & The M.G.'s, King Curtis, Santo & Johnny, Duke Ellington, The Drifter and Andy Williams—and was used i numerous films, including the 1995 hi *Mr. Holland's Opus*.

This solo is basically the melody c the song. Play it with a breathy, wid vibrato, utilizing a classical tone an technique. Employ a very light tongu articulation.

Vital Stats

Clarinet player: Acker Bilk

Song: "Stranger on the Shore"

Album: single release

Age at time of recording: 33

Clarinet used: unknown

Mouthpiece: unknown

from FLAMINGO KID
Words by Robert Mellin
Music by Acker Bilk

Here's a famous Beatles song that features a clarinet trio.

Robert Burns (1st clarinet)

Robert (Bob) Burns was born in Toronto, Ontario (Canada) in 1923. During World War II, he was a member of the Canadian Central Air Force Band, which took him to Great Britain. After the war, he stayed and became a popular clarinet, alto sax, and tenor sax player. An impressive 50-year recording career meant playing with artists like Roy Eldridge, Annie Ross, Benny Goodman, Barbra Streisand, Guy Lombardo, The Manhattan Transfer, Ted Heath, and of course The Beatles. Burns appeared in several British television series, including *Off the Record* and *Jazz 625*; he was chosen to play in an all-star band for the TV movie *Love You Madly: A Salute to Duke Ellington* in 1969. He continued to perform regularly with small groups in jazz clubs throughout the 1970s; in the late 1980s, he returned to Canada. Burns died in 2000.

Henry MacKenzie (2nd clarinet)

Henry Mackay Mackenzie was born on February 15, 1923 in Edinburgh, Scotland. He began music studies on the accordion, later settling on the saxophone and clarinet. He played in various bands in his native Edinburgh before being called up for duty in an army band during the war, where he served five years. In 1949, his solo clarinet playing attracted British bandleader Ted Heath, who offered him a job with his group in London. Mackenzie remained in Heath's band for 18 years, playing tenor saxophone in the section and solo clarinet, tracking 23 albums with Heath, plus numerous recordings with other groups. After Heath's death in 1969, Mackenzie branched out into session work as a first-call musician for Henry Mancini, Billy May, and Nelson Riddle; he performed regularly with various groups on BBC Radio. Additionally, Mackenzie wrote and arranged music, making albums of atmospheric pieces that were used on soundtracks, including the 1980 film *The Babysitter*. He officially retired from music in 1995. Mackenzie died on September 2, 2007, in Carshalton, Surrey (U.K.).

Photo by National Jazz Archive/Heritage Images/Getty Images

Henry Mackenzie

Kenny Baker (trumpet), Danny Moss (saxophone) and Henry Mackenzie (clarinet) in rehearsal with Billy May at the BBC recording studios, London, 22 April 1982.

Frank Reidy (bass clarinet)

Frank Reidy was born on November 26, 1919. He was one of the premier reed doublers in Great Britain from the 1950s through the 1980s. In his early years, he backed Peter Sellers and Spike Milligan on their *Goon Show* broadcasts. But his greatest exposure was as the tenor saxophone "voice" for the character "Zoot" on *The Muppet Show*, where he was featured on all 120 episodes. Reidy also was the musician contractor for EMI Recording Studios. He died in February 1996 in Camden, London.

Burns, Mackenzie, and Reidy played together on numerous occasions, both before and after the historic Beatles session. All three were featured in many music magazine ads with the instruments they endorsed.

The Beatles

The Beatles are the best-selling music act of all time, with estimated sales of 600 million units worldwide. Originally called the Quarrymen, they formed in Liverpool, England, with main members Paul McCartney (see page 41), John Lennon, George Harrison, and Ringo Starr. They hold the record for the most No. 1 albums on the U.K. Albums Chart (15), most No. 1 hits on the Billboard Hot 100 chart (20), and most singles sold in the U.K. (21.9 million). The band has received seven Grammy Awards, four Brit Awards, an Academy Award (for Best Original Song Score for the 1970 film *Let It Be*) and 15 Ivor Novello Awards.

"It was really an arbitrary number when I wrote ['When I'm Sixty-Four']. I probably should have called it 'When I'm 65,' which is the retirement age in England. And the rhyme would have been easy, 'something, something alive when I'm 65.' But it felt too predictable. It sounded better to say 64."

–Paul McCartney

Photo Courtesy of National Jazz Archive United Kingdom and the Les Tomkins estate

Frank Reidy & Bob Burns
First-call London studio musicians recording with Quincy Jones, Henry Mancini and conductor Bob Farnon in April 1964; back row (L–R): Frank Reidy, Bob Burns (clarinet), Cecil James, Anthony Judd (bassoons); front row: Johnny Scott, Phil Goody, Geoffrey Gilbert (flutes), Leon Goossens (oboe)

They were installed into the Rock & Roll Hall of Fame in 1988, and all four main members were inducted individually between 1994 and 2015. In 2004 and 2011, the group topped Rolling Stone magazine's lists of the greatest artists in history, and Time magazine named them among the 20th century's 100 most important people. Some of their best-loved songs include "Yesterday," "I Want to Hold Your Hand," "A Day in the Life," and "Hey Jude." They are easily one of the greatest and most influential bands of all time, especially their innovations in songwriting, production, and recording.

How to Play It

Sgt. Pepper's Lonely Hearts Club Band was The Beatles' eighth studio album, released on May 26, 1967. It spent 27 weeks at No. 1 in the United Kingdom and 15 weeks at No. 1 on the U.S. Billboard Top LPs chart in 1967. Written by Paul McCartney, "When I'm Sixty-Four" is the ninth song on the album. According to McCartney, "I wrote it when I was about 15. Back then, I wasn't necessarily looking to be a rock 'n' roller. When I wrote 'When I'm Sixty-Four,' I thought I was writing a song for Sinatra."

During the mixing stage, the decision was made to speed up the song, raising it by a half step, primarily to make Paul sound like a "16-year-old looking forward to being 64." If you slow down the recording and bring it down a half step, you can hear it at the original speed and key signature, which was C major.

The solo is the whole clarinet trio score for two B♭ clarinets and one bass clarinet. Swing all the eighth notes, and use a straight tone throughout; no vibrato.

Vital Stats

Clarinet players: Robert Burns, Henry MacKenzie, Frank Reidy

Song: "When I'm Sixty-Four"

Album: *Sgt. Pepper's Lonely Hearts Club Band*

Age at time of recording: unknown

Clarinet Used: unknown

Mouthpiece: unknown

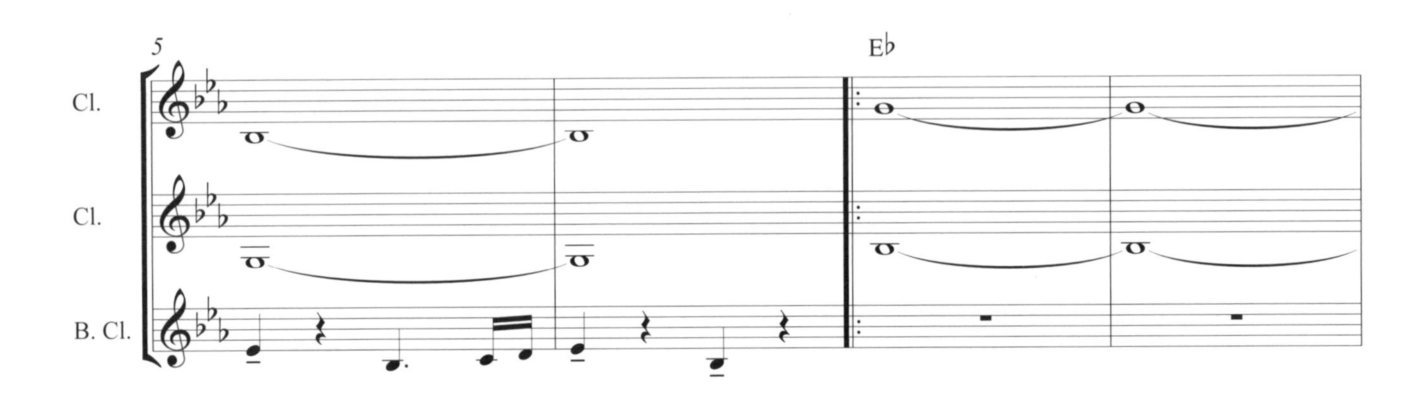

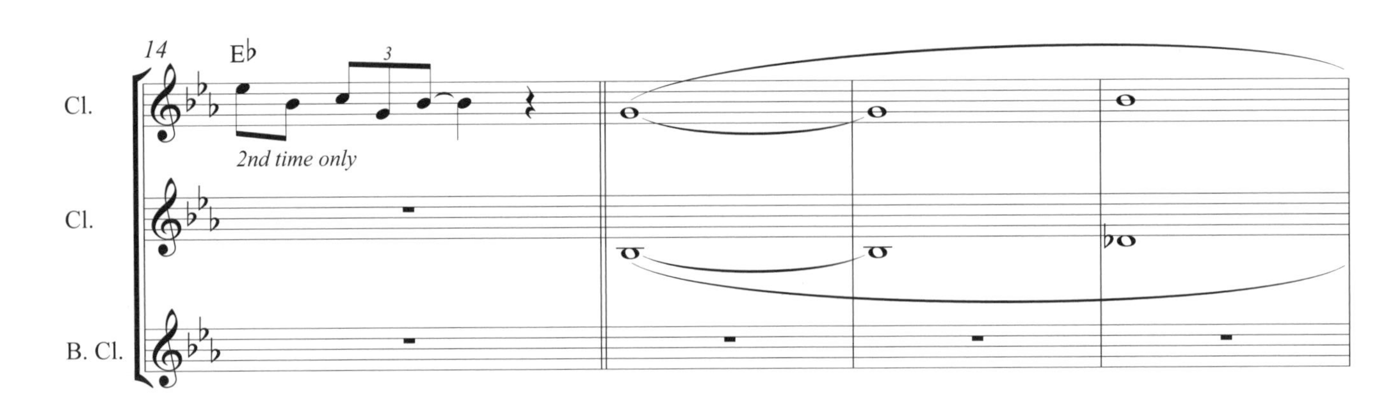

Words and Music by John Lennon and Paul McCartney

18
Ab
Cl.
Cl.
B. Cl.
Bb
Cm
F
Bb7
22
Eb
Cm
Bb
3
3
26
Cm
G7
31
Cm
Fm
Ab
36
Bb
Eb
Bb

40
E♭
B♭7
Cl.
Cl.
B. Cl.
44
E♭
48
A♭
52
B♭
Cm
F
B♭7
E♭
56
A♭
B♭
E♭

Henry Diltz

Henry Diltz
American folk music revival group the Modern Folk Quartet in concert at the Night Owl in New York City, 1966. From left to right, Henry Diltz, Jerry Yester and Chip Douglas

"Music is a huge part of just being a human being... being alive!"
–Henry Diltz

Although not one of the famous Monkees' hits, this song nevertheless features a great clarinet solo.

Henry Stanford Diltz was born on September 6, 1938 in Kansas City, Missouri. He started out on the harmonica, then switched to banjo and clarinet. Diltz studied psychology in college while in Hawaii, and formed the band Modern Folk Quartet, who eventually made two albums for Warner Bros. While a member of that ensemble, Diltz grew interested in photography, and soon became popular in that field as well. His "fly-on-the-wall" style portraits made him famous for his photos and album covers, including works of the Eagles, Neil Young, Crosby Stills & Nash, Jackson Browne, America, Steppenwolf, James Taylor, and Jimi Hendrix. He was the official photographer at the Woodstock festival in August 1969.

At one point, he was hired by *Tiger Beat* magazine to photograph the band The Monkees. Quickly becoming friends with the band, he began touring with them, recording clarinet and harmonica parts on some of their recordings.

As a music photographer, he is responsible for more than 250 album covers and thousands of publicity shots in the 1960s and '70s. His work has appeared in *The New York Times, Los Angeles Times, LIFE, People, Rolling Stone, High Times,* and *Billboard.* Today, Diltz has several galleries devoted to his photography career.

The Monkees

The Monkees were an American rock and pop band, originally active between 1966 and 1971. The initial line-up consisted of actor/musicians Micky Dolenz, Davy Jones, Michael Nesmith, and Peter Tork. The group was conceived in 1965 by television producers Bob Rafelson and Bert Schneider, specifically for the situation comedy series *The Monkees*, which aired from 1966 to 1968. While limited to roles in the recording studio, they all contributed lead vocals to various tracks. Their TV show won two Emmy Awards, and is still in heavy syndication. They have sold more than 75 million records worldwide, making them one of the biggest-selling groups of all time. Their international hits include "Last Train to Clarksville," "I'm a Believer," "Pleasant Valley Sunday," and "Daydream Believer."

How to Play It

"Shake 'Em Up" was written by the powerhouse songwriting team of Jerry Leiber and Mike Stoller. First recorded in 1967 by American doo-wop and early rock 'n' roll group The Coasters, The Monkees' version was never released as a single.

This is basically a rock 'n' roll-style clarinet solo. Swing and tongue all the notes. Measure 16, beat 3 has a glissando fall to the G. It kind of sounds like a bad note left in.

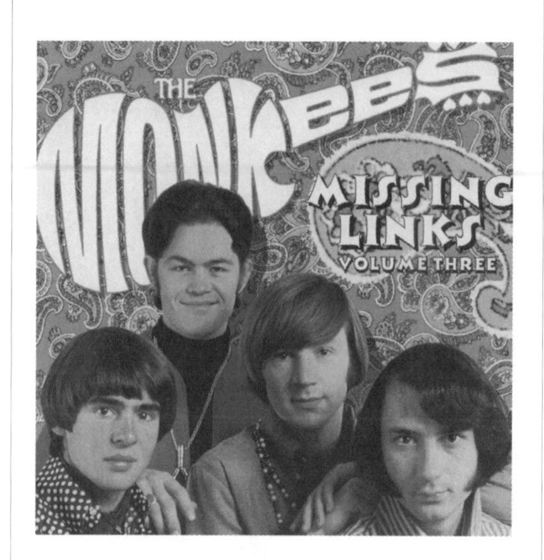

Vital Stats

Clarinet player: Henry Diltz

Song: "Shake 'Em Up"

Album: *Missing Links, Volume Three*

Age at time of recording: 30

Clarinet used: unknown

Mouthpiece: unknown

Words and Music by Jerry Leiber and Mike Stoller

Sermon Posthumas

A mysterious, unknown soloist plays the bass clarinet on this song.

Graham Nash

Graham William Nash was born on February 2, 1942 in Blackpool, Lancashire (U.K.). He started playing music as a teenager, picking up the guitar during the mid-1950s. In 1955, he and his schoolmate Allan Clarke formed the Two Teens. They were a successful duo that went through different band names and inclinations, finally dubbing themselves The Hollies, as a salute to their hero Buddy Holly. Signing with EMI in 1963, The Hollies had their first U.K. Top 10, "Stay." Other hits came, including "We're Through," "I'm Alive," "Look Through Any Window," "Bus Stop," "Just One Look," and "(Ain't That) Just Like Me." With the later addition of Tony Hicks, they became known for their distinctive three-part vocal harmony style. During a 1966 Hollies U.S. tour, Nash met both David Crosby and Stephen Stills. They soon formed the now-famous Crosby, Stills & Nash. The trio's first album, *Crosby, Stills & Nash*, was released in May 1969 and featured two hits: "Suite: Judy Blue Eyes" and "Marrakesh Express." The album sold four million copies. Other hit albums include *Deja Vu, 4 Way Street*, and the greatest-hits album *So Far*.

Nash has released six solo albums, and was inducted into the Rock & Roll Hall of Fame in 1997 as a member of Crosby, Stills & Nash and as a member of The Hollies in 2010. He's also been a successful photographer, resulting in many successful exhibitions and publications of his works.

Graham Nash
Graham Nash backstage at the Frost Amphitheater, Stanford CA, Spring 1976

"I wasn't thinking of the longevity of any of my songs, but I am extremely pleased with the lasting effect."
–Graham Nash

How to Play It

Songs for Beginners was Nash's debut solo studio album, released in May 1971. It peaked at No. 15 on the Billboard Top Pop Albums chart, and was certified as a gold record by the RIAA. The single "Chicago" made it to No. 35 on the Billboard Hot 100.

"Better Days" features a bass clarinet solo by unknown Sermon Posthumas. Played on bass clarinet, the solo stays in the high range of the instrument; this can be difficult for beginners. Use vibrato throughout, and employ note bends on all high Cs.

Vital Stats

Clarinet player: Sermon Posthumas

Song: "Better Days"

Album: *Songs for Beginners*

Age at time of recording: unknown

Clarinet used: unknown

Mouthpiece: unknown

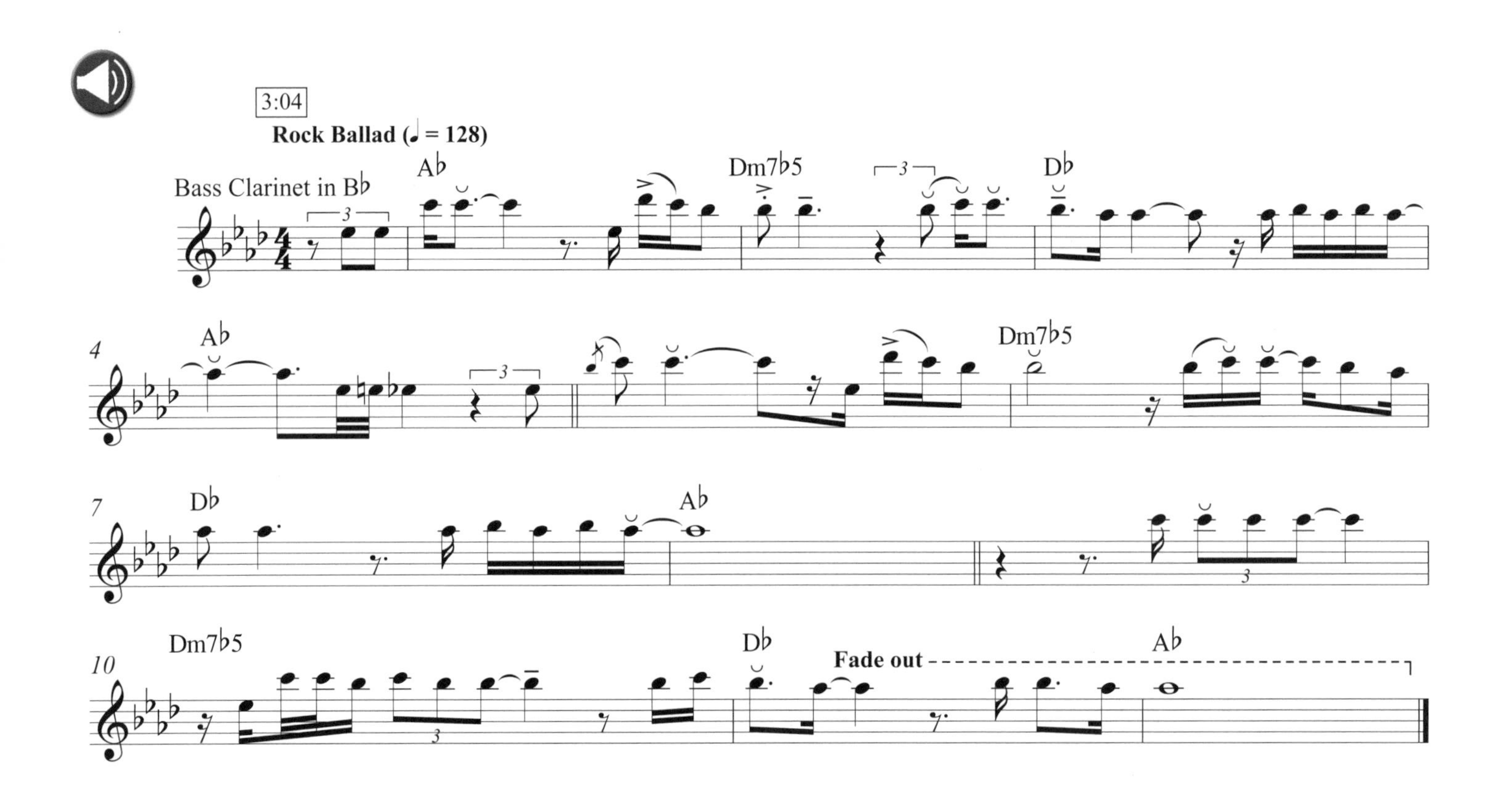

Words and Music by Graham Nash

Soloist information is unknown.

to by Michael Putland/Getty Images

Paul McCartney

"I was depressed. You would be. You were breaking from your lifelong friends. I wanted to get back to square one, so I ended up forming Wings."

–Paul McCartney

Paul McCartney

Paul McCartney shows that he can make any band be successful.

James Paul McCartney was born on June 18, 1942 in Liverpool, Lancashire (U.K.). His father was a trumpet player and pianist who encouraged Paul to take piano lessons. Learning piano by ear, he received a trumpet from his father for his 14th birthday, but traded it for an acoustic guitar, reversing the order of the strings and playing it left-handed. (Self-taught, he eventually became proficient on bass, guitar, keyboards, and drums.) McCartney wrote his first song, "I Lost My Little Girl," and composed another early tune on piano that would become "When I'm Sixty-Four" (see page 32). In 1957, McCartney began his career as a member of the Quarrymen, which evolved into The Beatles (see page 32) in 1960. He gained worldwide fame as vocalist and bassist and with John Lennon, formed one of the most popular and successful songwriting teams in music history. His Beatles songs "And I Love Her," "Yesterday," "Eleanor Rigby," "Hey Jude," and "Blackbird" are just some of his most famous. After the group disbanded in 1970, he pursued a solo career with the album *McCartney*, then formed the band Wings.

McCartney has written or co-written 32 songs that have reached No. 1 on the Billboard Hot 100. He was twice inducted into the Rock & Roll Hall of Fame (as a member of the Beatles and as a solo artist), boasts 18 Grammy Awards, and received a knighthood in 1997 for services to music. Sir Paul remains one of the most successful composers and performers of all time.

Wings

Paul McCartney and Wings (also known by their original name Wings) were formed in 1971 by McCartney, his wife Linda McCartney on keyboards, session drummer Denny Seiwell, and former Moody Blues guitarist Denny Laine. McCartney's third solo album became the first Wings album, *Wild Life*. The band's third album, *Band on the Run*, hosted two Top 10 singles, "Jet" and the title track. In 1977, McCartney dissolved Wings and resumed his solo career shortly afterward. In the end, Wings had 12 Top 10 singles (one No. 1) in the U.K. and 14 Top 10 singles (including six No. 1s) in the U.S.

How to Play It

Band on the Run was the third studio album by Paul McCartney and Wings, released in December 1973. It was McCartney's fifth album after leaving the Beatles in April 1970. It remains his most successful album and the most celebrated of his post-Beatles works.

This solo sounds like a Swing-era, Benny Goodman-style solo, especially the lick in measure 6! Remember to add vibrato, and use jazz articulations.

Vital Stats

Clarinet Player: unknown

Song: "Nineteen Hundred and Eighty-Five"

Album: *Band on the Run*

Age at time of recording: unknown

Clarinet used: unknown

Mouthpiece: unknown

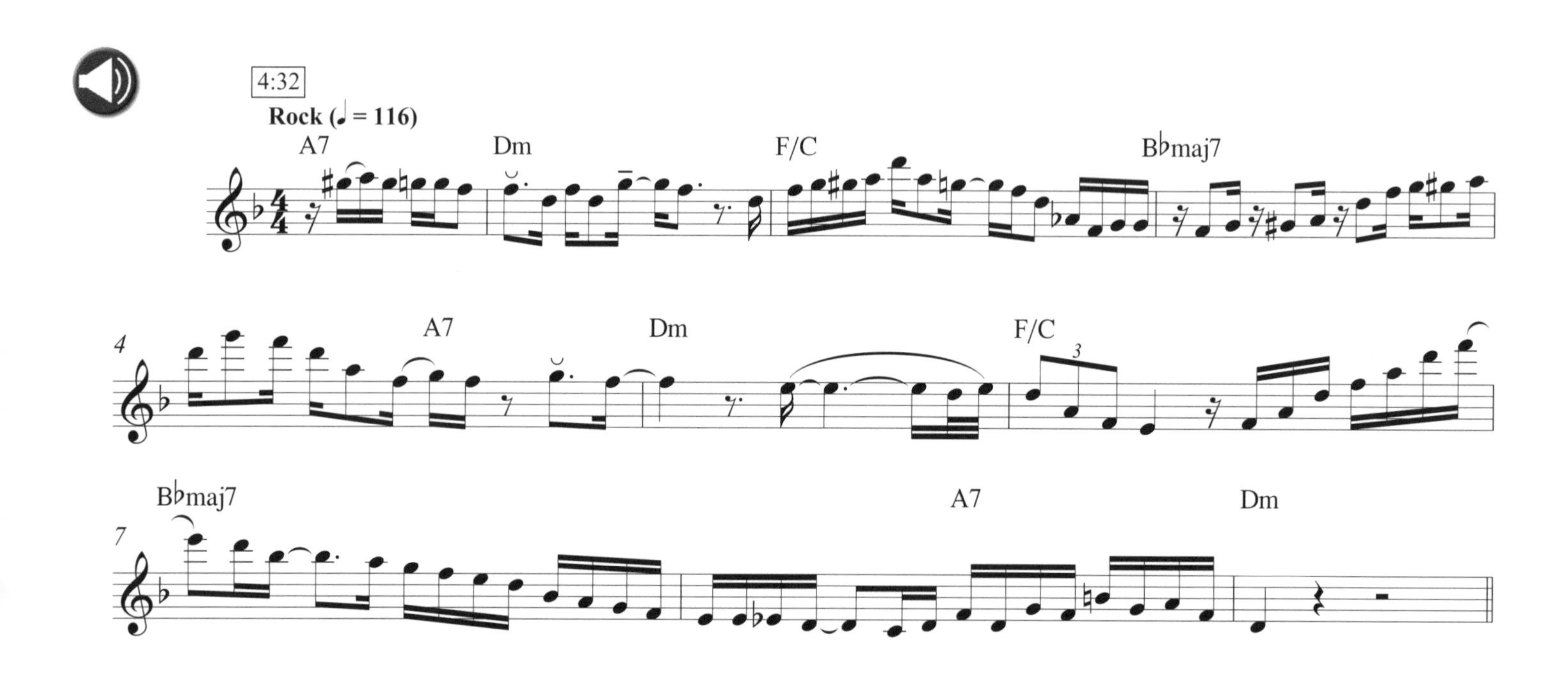

Words and Music by Paul and Linda McCartney

Richie Cannata

Richie Cannata was *the* woodwind voice of Billy Joel!

Richie Cannata was born on March 3, 1949 in Brooklyn, New York. He started playing piano at age four and by six was playing clarinet. When he moved to tenor sax at age eight, he never looked back! He played his first gig at age 13 and went on to play in school bands and with local musicians. Perfecting his skills as a live performer and studio musician, he played flute, clarinet, keyboards, and all the saxes. Cannata joined Billy Joel's band in 1975, playing solos on "Scenes from an Italian Restaurant," "Say Goodbye to Hollywood," "It's Still Rock and Roll to Me," and "New York State of Mind." After leaving the band in 1981, he opened Cove City Sound Studios in Glen Cove, New York, where Celine Dion, Billy Joel, Jennifer Lopez, and Marc Anthony (among others) have recorded.

Cannata played in Tommy Shaw's band in the mid-1980s, performing on Shaw's first three solo albums. He also played for Taylor Dayne in the late 1980s/early 1990s, and was a saxophonist with Bernie Williams. From 1991 to 1998, Cannata toured with The Beach Boys, where he played woodwinds and synthesizers. In 2006, Cannata briefly toured again with Joel, and was part of his record-setting 12-show run at Madison Square Garden. In December 2013, Cannata and Sean J. Kennedy's educational jazz improv play-along series *Improvising and Soloing in the Pocket* was released by Carl Fischer Music to critical acclaim. The series includes books for all instruments, and features music from Cannata's 2011 solo album *Richie Cannata*.

Photo by Michael Ochs Archives/Getty Images

Richie Cannata & Billy Joel
Singer/songwriter Billy Joel poses for a portrait with his band in circa 1977.
(L-R) Liberty DeVito, Doug Stegmeyer, Billy Joel, Richie Cannata

> ***"I followed the lyric of the song and kept it in a New Orleans style. I did the solos and ad-libs in only one or two takes."***
> –Richie Cannata

Cannata and ex-Joel-mates Liberty DeVitto and Russell Javors formed The Lords of 52nd Street, an ensemble devoted to creating faithful renditions of recorded Joel originals.

Billy Joel

William Martin (Billy) Joel was born on May 9, 1949 in the Bronx, New York. Growing up, he took piano lessons at the insistence of his mother. After dropping out of high school to pursue a musical career, he released his first solo album, *Cold Spring Harbor*, in 1971. In 1972, Joel caught the attention of Columbia Records after a live radio performance of the song "Captain Jack" became popular in Philadelphia. He signed a record deal with the company and released his second album, *Piano Man*, in 1973.

His critical and commercial breakthrough album, *The Stranger*, was released in 1977, selling over 10 million copies, and spawning several hit singles, including "Just the Way You Are," "Movin' Out (Anthony's Song)," "Only the Good Die Young," "She's Always a Woman," and Joel's favorite, "Scenes from an Italian Restaurant." Known as the Piano Man, Joel is one of the best-selling music artists of all time, with over 150 million records sold worldwide. He's had 33 Top 40 hits (with three No. 1 hits) and 23 Grammy nominations. In 1999, he was inducted into the Rock & Roll Hall of Fame.

How to Play It

The Stranger was Joel's fifth studio album, released on Columbia Records in September 1977. Although never offered as a single, "Scenes from an Italian Restaurant" has become one of Joel's favorite compositions, both personally and among fans.

The song features five sections; one is a Dixieland-style segment, from which the solo is taken. Make sure to swing and tongue all your sixteenth notes, and feel the heavy downbeats. Think Dixieland clarinet! The harmony parts are written out in measures 17-18.

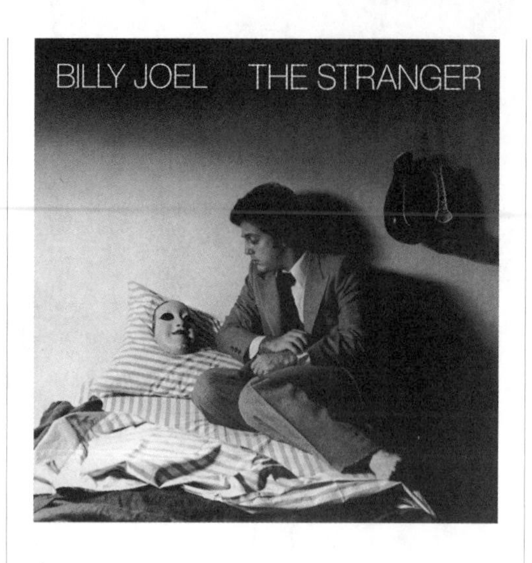

Vital Stats

Clarinet player: Richie Cannata

Song: "Scenes from an Italian Restaurant"

Album: *The Stranger*

Age at time of recording: 28

Clarinet used: Leblanc

Mouthpiece: unknown

Words and Music by Billy Joel

Jim Rothermel

Jim Rothermel

Jim Rothermel was born into a Navy family in Panama on September 29, 1941. His first instrument was the harmonica, which he began playing in the fifth grade. His father bought him a clarinet two years later, adding saxophone and other wind instruments in high school. By the time he was 17, Jim was working as a professional musician. He has played with artists like Jesse Colin Young, Boz Scaggs, Jerry Garcia, Bucky Pizzarelli, Charlie Byrd, Jay McShann, Buddy DeFranco, Charles Brown, and Van Morrison. Rothermel has been featured on over 100 albums, spread over many genres—mainly jazz, swing, Dixieland, and rock. He was an active part of the San Francisco music scene for 30 years, and appeared on the 1987 Grammy Award-winning album *A Tribute to Steve Goodman.*

Rothermel also taught saxophone at Sonoma State University, a job that included working with students in the Bay Area Music in the Schools program. Additionally, he was a guest artist in clinics at Santa Rosa and Delta junior colleges. Jim put out one album, *Memories of You.*

Rothermel died of complications from leukemia on May 16, 2011.

"I think the more the listener can contribute to the song, the better; the more they become part of the song, and they fill in the blanks."
–John Prine

John Prine

John Edward Prine was born on October 10, 1946 in Maywood, Illinois. He started playing guitar at 14, including old folk tunes taught to him by his brother Dave; he also attended classes at Chicago's Old Town School of Folk Music. After serving in West Germany with the U.S. Army, he returned to Chicago in the late 1960s, where he worked as a mailman. Writing and singing songs were just a hobby at first, but he became a club performer as a member of Chicago's folk revival.

Prine credits film critic Roger Ebert and singer-songwriter Kris Kristofferson for discovering him, resulting in the production of Prine's self-titled debut album with Atlantic Records in 1971. Several songs from the album became both his signature tunes and folk and country standards: "Illegal Smile," "Sam Stone," "Angel from Montgomery," and "Paradise." In 2020, *John Prine* was ranked No.149 on *Rolling Stone* magazine's list of the 500 greatest albums of all time. He recorded three more albums for Atlantic, later signing with Asylum Records. In 1981, he co-founded Oh Boy Records, an independent label on which he released most of his subsequent albums. Prine won his first Grammy for the 1991 album, *The Missing Years*. In 2003, he joined the Nashville Songwriters Hall of Fame, while his 1971 eponymous album was inducted into the Grammy Hall of Fame in 2014.

Prine died on April 7, 2020 in Nashville, from complications related to COVID-19.

How to Play It

Bruised Orange was released in 1978, and was Prine's fifth album. Time signature 7/4, or alternating measures of 3/4 and 4/4? Either way, do your best to read the meter changes, remembering that the quarter-note pulse remains constant. The clarinet solo has a pretty tone, so give it a classical-like sound. All tonguing should be light and legato. In measure 4, lay way back on the triplets, and add vibrato on the last note.

Vital Stats

Clarinet player: Jim Rothermel

Song: "Sabu Visits the Twin Cities Alone"

Album: *Bruised Orange*

Age at time of recording: 37

Clarinet used: unknown

Mouthpiece: unknown

Words and Music by John Prine

John Helliwell

"On 'Take the Long Way Home' the clarinet's duet with Rick Davis's harmonica seems to veer towards a Dixieland vibe."

–John Helliwell on "Take the Long Way Home"

John Helliwell

It's quite possible you could hear these next two John Helliwell clarinet solos on the radio today!

John Anthony Helliwell was born on February 15, 1945 in Todmorden, West Yorkshire (U.K). At age nine, he sang in the church choir and took piano lessons for a year. Inspired by English clarinetist Monty Sunshine, he bought a clarinet when he was 13, taking up saxophone two years later. After completing high school, Helliwell worked as a computer programmer, playing with various bands and groups, including The Dicemen and Jugs O'Henry. He turned professional in 1965, performing with The Alan Bown Set. In 1973, he got a call from Supertramp member Dougie Thomson, asking him to join the band. Soon, he was recording the album *Crime of the Century*.

Along with playing the famous sax solo on "The Logical Song," and clarinet solos on "Take the Long Way Home" and "Breakfast in America," he recorded and toured with Supertramp all the way into the 1990s, when the band went on hiatus. Helliwell also played on Pink Floyd's album *A Momentary Lapse of Reason*, French singer Jean-Jacques Goldman's album *Positif*, and clarinet on Sara Hickman's 1990 album, *Shortstop*. In 2004, Helliwell formed the band Crème Anglaise with Mark Hart, contributed saxophone work on the Simon Apple album *River to the Sea*, and lent clarinet to The Pineapple Thief's song "Fend for Yourself," released in 2016. Helliwell currently fronts the Super Big Tramp Band, playing versions of Supertramp tunes arranged by members of the band. He released the album *Ever Open Door* in October 2020, which features ballads with saxophone and clarinet, along with a string quartet and Hammond organ.

Richard Davies

Richard (Rick) Davies was born on July 22, 1944 in Swindon, Wiltshire, England. He got into music at the age of eight, when his parents gave him a secondhand radiogram. At the age of 12, he joined the British Railways Staff Association Brass and Silver Jubilee Band as a snare drummer. He later self-taught himself keyboards. In 1962, while studying in the art department at Swindon College, he formed his own band, called Rick's Blues. In August 1969, Davies decided to form a new band, and returned home from Switzerland to place an ad in the music magazine *Melody Maker*. Roger Hodgson auditioned, and they quickly formed a music friendship and began writing music together. That first band was initially called Daddy, but later

renamed Supertramp in January 1970. He wrote and co-wrote the majority of Supertramp's songs, including those of their 1979 hit album "Breakfast in America." He shared lead vocals often with Roger Hodgson, whose deep baritone voice occasionally sang in falsetto on songs such as on "Goodbye Stranger" and "My Kind of Lady." After Hodgson's departure in 1983, Davies kept Supertramp for five more years until it was disbanded in 1988. In 1997, during work on what would have been his first solo album, Davies decided to re-form Supertramp. The group promptly returned to recording and touring, which yielded another two studio albums before they split again but reunited in 2010 for their 70–10 tour. Davies currently owns Rick Davies Productions and is the copyright holder of Supertramp's recordings.

How to Play It

Breakfast in America is Supertramp's sixth studio album, released on March 29, 1979. It contained four hit songs: "The Logical Song," "Goodbye Stranger," "Take the Long Way Home," and "Breakfast in America." It won two Grammy Awards—for Best Album Package and Best Engineered Non-Classical Recording—and has sold more than four million copies in the U.S. and more than three million in France.

"Take the Long Way Home" was the fourth single from the album. It reached No. 10 on the U.S. charts and is still on heavy rotation on the radio today.

The solo is very much in the Dixieland style, especially its call-and-response with the harmonica. Swing all the notes with an aggressive tongue attack, and blow hard. In measure 5, hit that high F solidly and add a quick glissando downward before beat 2, playing the jazz articulations on beats 2, 3, and 4.

Vital Stats

Clarinet player: John Helliwell

Song: "Take the Long Way Home"

Album: *Breakfast in America*

Age at time of recording: 34

Clarinet used: Buffet R13

Mouthpiece: James Kanter

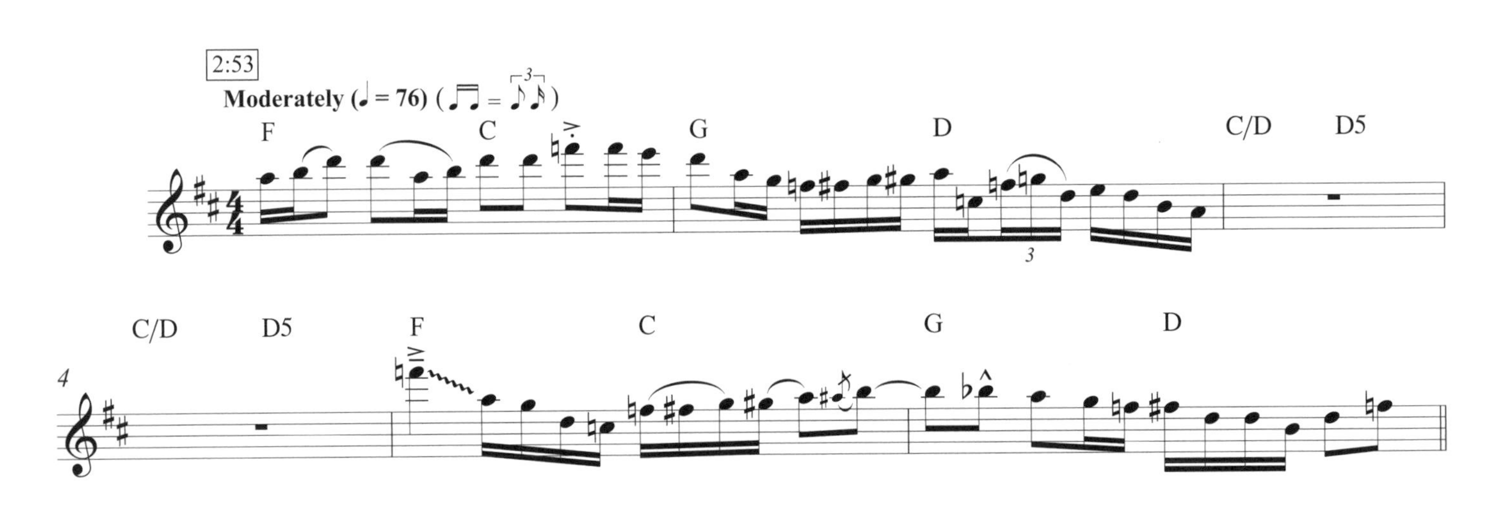

Words and Music by Rick Davies and Roger Hodgson

John Helliwell

See Helliwell bio on page 47.

Supertramp

Supertramp was formed in London in 1970. They got their name from the W.H. Davies' book *The Autobiography of a Super-Tramp* (published in 1908). Signed to A&M Records, their album *Crime of the Century* went to No. 1 in the U.K., and they reached their commercial peak with 1979's *Breakfast in America*. In 1983, lead singer Roger Hodgson left the group to pursue a solo career. They still perform today with various configurations.

As of 2019, Supertramp has sold more than 71.2 million records.

How to Play It

The two clarinet solos can described as "klezmer," according to Helliwell. There are two solo sections:

Solo 1

Play with lots of vibrato, and use an "oh" embouchure for the correct tone. In measure 1, scoop that C♯. The A to B♭ notes in measures 3-4 lend the solo a bluesy sound.

Solo 2

This solo is much busier. Use a note scoop on the A♭ in measure 2; do the same on the F in measure 4, beat 4. Measure 5 has a fast, left-side key line that might need practice. Measure 7 needs a jaw bend down on the E to C♯, with a scoop on that C♯. In measure 8, hit the high F with an accent and note scoop.

Vital Stats

Clarinet player: John Helliwell

Song: "Breakfast in America"

Album: *Breakfast in America*

Age at time of recording: 34

Clarinet used: Buffet R13

Mouthpiece: James Kanter

> *"With the 'oom-pah-pah' of the tuba/trombone on* **Breakfast in America,** *my playing unconsciously gravitated to a sort of klezmer-type sound—not to have been repeated since!"*
>
> –John Helliwell on "Breakfast in America"

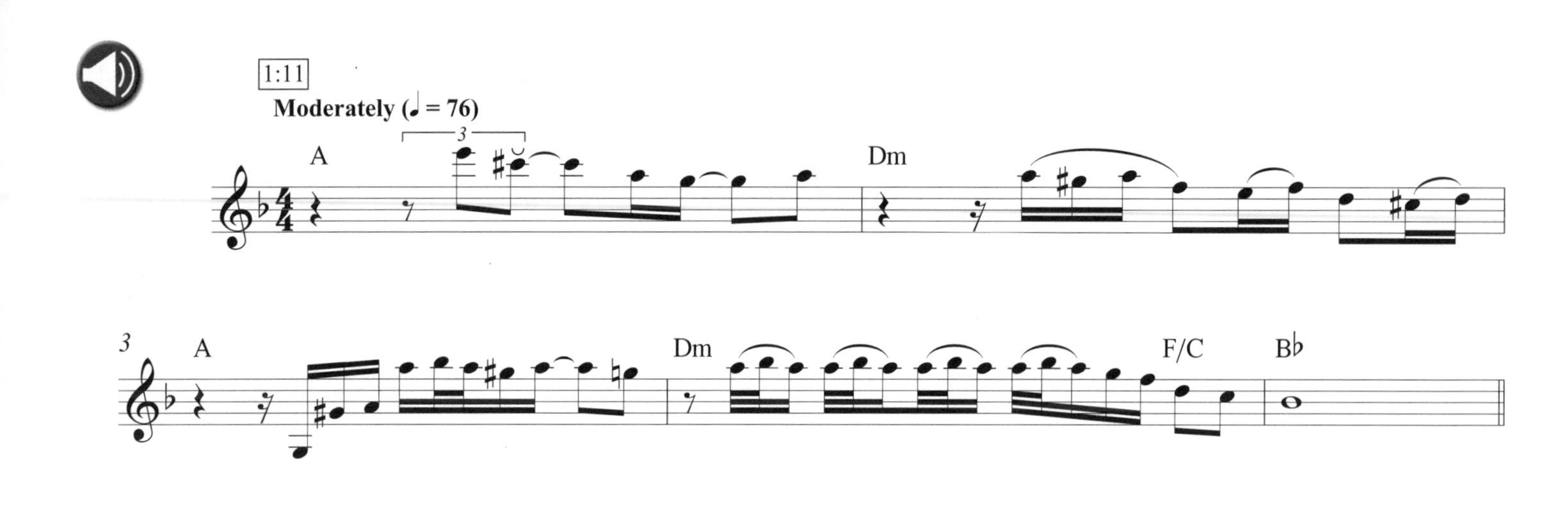

Words and Music by Rick Davies and Roger Hodgson

Debbie Harry
Blondie in 1977: Gary Valentine, Clem Burke, Debbie Harry, Chris Stein, and Jimmy Destri

Soloist information in unknown.

Deborah Harry

Deborah Ann Harry was born Angela Trimble on July 1, 1945 in Miami, Florida. Adoptive parents rechristened her Deborah Harry, raising her as their own. In 1965, she graduated from junior college with an associate of arts degree. Her odd jobs included secretarial work for the BBC, waiting tables, and an infamous nine-month stint as a Playboy bunny. Harry began her musical career as a backing singer for the folk-rock group The Wind in the Willows in the late 1960s.

In 1974, she and her boyfriend, guitarist Chris Stein, formed the band Blondie in New York City. Their debut album was released in 1976. They gained big success with their 1978 album *Parallel Lines*, which spawned six singles, including the No. 1 hit "Heart of Glass." In 1981, Harry released her debut solo album, *KooKoo*. She also pursued an acting career, with roles in the films *Union City* (1980) and *Videodrome* (1983). Her second solo album, *Rockbird*, came out in 1986, with two more solo albums later. She landed more film roles, including *Body Bags, Heavy*, and *Tales from the Darkside: The Movie.* Blondie was reunited in the late 1990s, recording *No Exit* in 1999, followed by *The Curse of Blondie*. The band's 11th studio album, *Pollinator*, charted at No. 4 in the United Kingdom in 2017.

Harry's autobiography, *Face It*, was published in October 2019.

> *"The Blondie character I created was always meant to be androgynous."*
> –Debbie Harry

Blondie

Blondie was co-founded by singer Debbie Harry and guitarist Chris Stein, who became pioneers in New York City's American punk and New Wave music scene of the mid/late-1970s.

The band was seen as an underground band until the release of *Parallel Lines* (1978), which featured "Heart of Glass." Over the next three years, the ensemble achieved several hit singles, including "Call Me," "Rapture," and "The Tide Is High." Blondie disbanded after putting out its sixth studio album, *The Hunter* (1982), as Harry continued a solo career.

The group re-formed in 1997, achieving renewed success with "Maria" (1999) becoming a No. 1 single in the U.K.—exactly 20 years after their first U.K. No. 1 single "Heart of Glass." The band toured and performed throughout the world, and was inducted into the Rock & Roll Hall of Fame in 2006. Blondie has sold nearly 40 million records worldwide and is still active, with the band's 11th studio album, *Pollinator*, released in May 2017.

How to Play It

Autoamerican (November 1980) is the fifth studio album from Blondie. It reached No. 7 in the U.S., and contained two hit singles, "The Tide Is High" and "Rapture." This jazz track was a huge departure for the band. Regretfully, we don't know who played this swinging solo.

Swing all the notes, lay back on the beat, and play the notated scoops. Make sure you practice and are comfortable in the key of F♯!

Vital Stats

Clarinet Player: unknown

Song: "Here's Looking at You"

Album: *Autoamerican*

Age at time of recording: unknown

Clarinet used: unknown

Mouthpiece: unknown

Words and Music by Deborah Harry and Chris Stein

Jan Van Halen

Jan Van Halen

Jan Van Halen was born on January 18, 1920 in Amsterdam, Netherlands. He caught the musical bug at a young age; by age 18, he was being declared a master of both the clarinet and the saxophone. Before he enlisted in the Dutch Air Force in 1939 to fight in World War II, Jan was playing in jazz bands, swing bands, and orchestras around Europe. His musical talents landed him a job playing marches for Dutch troops. When he was a captive soldier, he was assigned to entertain the troops and play propaganda music, rather than fight in the trenches.

After the war, Van Halen continued to work as a professional musician. His future, famous sons Alex and Edward were born in 1953 and 1955. Relocating to Pasadena, California, he continued to work as a musician, playing locally at The Continental Club, La Miranda Country Club, and The Alpine Haus. He often took on many different jobs to make ends meet, including janitorial work, washing dishes, and answering phones overnight. In 1972, he suffered the loss of one of his fingers, forcing him to play even less. With his last name now a famous brand, he was asked by the band Van Halen (at lead singer David Lee Roth's request) to blow a clarinet solo on the band's 1982 *Diver Down* album. The result brought him sudden notoriety, with his Dixie style solo on "Big Bad Bill (Is Sweet William Now)." In May 1986, he suffered a massive heart attack.

Jan Van Halen died on December 9, 1986 in Pasadena, California.

Van Halen

Van Halen was an American rock band formed in Pasadena, California in 1974. Original members include David Lee Roth, Michael Anthony, Eddie Van Halen, and drummer Alex Van Halen. The band's self-titled debut album reached No. 19 on the Billboard pop music charts and sold over 10 million copies in the U.S. The band released four more albums (*Van Halen II, Women and Children First, Fair Warning*, and *Diver Down*), all of which have since become certified multi-platinum. By the early 1980s, Van Halen was one of the most successful rock acts of the day. Their album 1984 was a huge commercial success, selling 10 million copies and hosting four hit singles. The lead, "Jump," was a No. 1 single.

In 1985, Roth left the band to embark on a solo career and was replaced by lead vocalist Sammy Hagar. With Hagar, the group released four U.S. No. 1, multi-platinum albums: *5150, OU812, For Unlawful Carnal Knowledge*, and *Balance* (1995). Hagar left the band in 1996, with former Extreme frontman Gary Cherone replacing him. Van Halen reunited with Hagar in 2003; they made a worldwide tour in 2004 and recorded the double-disc, greatest-hits collection *The Best of Both Worlds*. Hagar again

left Van Halen in 2005, as Roth returned the next year. In 2012, the band released their final studio album, *A Different Kind of Truth*, which was commercially and critically successful. It was the only album with Roth in 28 years, and featured Wolfgang Van Halen, Eddie's son, on bass, replacing Anthony.

They are one of only five rock bands with two studio albums to sell more than 10 million copies in the United States, and are tied for the most multi-platinum albums by an American band. As of March 2019, the band has sold 56 million albums in the States and more than 80 million worldwide. They can boast 13 No. 1 hits on Billboard's Mainstream Rock chart, and were inducted into the Rock & Roll Hall of Fame in 2007.

Founding guitarist Eddie Van Halen died of a stroke on October 6, 2020.

How to Play It

Diver Down was released on April 14, 1982, and spent 65 weeks on the album charts. It sold over four million copies in the United States.

"Big Bad Bill (Is Sweet William Now)" was written in 1924 with music by Milton Ager and lyrics by Jack Yellen. The song was a vocal hit for Margaret Young, an instrumental hit for the Don Clark Orchestra, and has been recorded many times—by Ernest Hare, Billy Murray, Glen Gray & the Casa Loma Orchestra, Peggy Lee, Merle Haggard, and Ry Cooder. Roth came across the song and it instantly made him think of having Jan Van Halen record the song with the band; it was the band's only song that featured him. A massive departure for Van Halen, the tune remains a time-tested fan favorite.

It's a Dixieland-style jazz solo, so swing all the notes with the jazz articulation, playing proper noted articulations.

Vital Stats

Clarinet player: Jan Van Halen

Song: "Big Bad Bill (Is Sweet William, Now)"

Album: *Diver Down*

Age at time of recording: 61

Clarinet used: unknown

Mouthpiece: unknown

"He was nervous, and we told him, 'Jan, just have a good time. We make mistakes! That's what makes it real.' I love what he did, but he was thinking back ten years ago when he was smokin', playing jazz and stuff. He played exactly what we wanted."

–Eddie Van Halen on "Big Bad Bill (Is Sweet William, Now)"

Lyric by Jack Yellen
Music by Milton Ager

Phil Woods

Alto sax legend Phil Woods shows the music world that he's also a world-class clarinet player!

Photo by Tom Copi/Michael Ochs Archives/Getty Images

Phil Woods

Philip Wells Woods was born November 2, 1931 in Springfield, Massachusetts. He began playing the alto saxophone at age 12; his first heroes were Benny Carter and Johnny Hodges. When he was 15, Phil studied with pianist Lennie Tristano in New York, later attending the Manhattan School of Music. Woods went to The Juilliard School as a clarinet major, and graduated in 1952. By the mid-50s, he was working alongside trumpeter Kenny Dorham and pianist George Wallington, and began playing with the big bands of Dizzy Gillespie, Buddy Rich, Thelonious Monk, and Quincy Jones. Moving to Europe in 1968, he became a popular artist—as a clarinetist, a bandleader, and a composer. Woods became best-known for recording his famous alto sax solo on Billy Joel's "Just the Way You Are" (1977); he also performed sax solos on Steely Dan's "Doctor Wu," from their album *Katy Lied* (1975), and on Paul Simon's "Have a Good Time," from *Still Crazy After All These Years* (also 1975). He's released over 50 solo albums, been nominated for 18 Grammy Awards (winning four), and has garnered Down Beat Awards over a dozen times, including the Down Beat Magazine Talent Deserving of Wider Recognition for Clarinet, way back in 1963.

Woods died of emphysema complications on September 29, 2015 in East Stroudsburg, Pennsylvania.

> *"The clarinet was a tough instrument. It was invented by people who never met each other."*
>
> –Phil Woods

Fats Navarro

How to Play It

"Nostalgia" was written by Fats Navarro. Based on the changes in "Out of Nowhere," it has become a favorite contrafact and jazz standard.

This solo is straight bebop, in a way only Phil Woods can play! Play the eighth-note lines with legato straight and the others swung. There are a lot of scoops throughout, including some in measures 6-7. Use vibrato on all notes that are of quarter-note duration and longer. Measures 23-24 have a brief quote of Dizzy Gillespie's "Hot House." In measure 24, play those notes straight.

Fats Navarro

Theodore "Fats" Navarro, Jr. was born on September 24, 1923 in Key West, Florida. His musical training began early, with piano lessons at age six; Fats began to take music seriously when, at age 13, he started playing the trumpet. He studied tenor sax and played it well enough to work briefly in the Walter Johnson band in Miami while still in high school. After graduating Frederick Douglass High School, he joined Sol Albright's band in Orlando, traveling with him to Cincinnati. While there, he received further trumpet lessons from an Ohio teacher, and soon went on the road with Snookum Russell's orchestra. Navarro also played in Andy Kirk's and Billy Eckstine's big bands. He worked and recorded with other well-known leaders, including Illinois Jacquet, Coleman Hawkins, Charlie Parker, and composer-bandleader Tadd Dameron in 1948.

Navarro died on July 6, 1950 in New York City.

Vital Stats

Clarinet player: Phil Woods

Song: "Nostalgia"

Album: *"Old Acquaintance" Conte Candoli with Phil Woods*

Age at time of recording: 55

Clarinet used: unknown

Mouthpiece: unknown

By Theodore (Fats) Navarro

33
Bm7 E7 Amaj7 Cm7
37
F7 Amaj7 C#m7
41
F#7b9 Bm7 F#7b9 Bm7
45
F7
3
3
48
Bm7 E7 Amaj7
3
51
Cm7 F7 Amaj7
55
C#m7 F#7b9
58
Bm7 F#7b9 Bm7 Dm7 G7
62
C#m7 Cdim7 Bm7 E7 Amaj7 Bm7 E7

Neil Buckley

Enya's unique music features an equally unique-sounding clarinet solo in "On Your Shore."

Neil Buckley was born in Dublin, Ireland on November 21, 1939. He was drawn to music at an early age, following his brother's interest in it. After high school, he worked in advertising rather than attending college. Buckley eventually bought his own clarinet and began teaching himself how to play, becoming engrossed in traditional jazz. He played with various bands in Dublin's jazz scene throughout the 1960s. One experience included a performance with legend Louis Armstrong, who was in Ireland on a goodwill visit from America. Neil assembled the band and called the experience "the proudest moment of my life." In the later '60s, he was the national road racing Motorbike champion. In the 1970s, Neil met John Dankworth and Cleo Laine and played with the George Gurring Quintet. He eventually qualified as a teacher and taught art and photography.

Neil Buckley and Louis Armstrong

After meeing Pól, Ciarán, Moya, and Enya Brennan, a family of musicians who became the band Clannad, Buckley was asked to play on a track of their 1982 album *Fuaim*; he toured with them as well. When Enya left the band and recorded her first album, Neil was asked to play on it.

With the Neil Buckley Quintet, Neil established himself in the jazz scene in Northern Ireland, and released a single called "Ice Cream," previously recorded by Chris Barber and his Jazz Band. As a saxophonist and clarinetist, he kept a low profile, never craving the limelight.

Buckley died of multiple myloma on August 10, 2010.

Enya

Eithne Pádraigín Ní Bhraonáin (Enya Patricia Brennan) was born on May 17, 1961 in Gweedore, County Donegal, Ireland. She began piano lessons at age four, developing a taste for classical music at age 11. She left school at 17 and studied classical music in college for one year, with the aim of becoming a piano teacher. In 1980, she began her music career after joining her family's Celtic

Enya
Clannad with Enya (seated, right)

> *"I was studying classical music. I had a background in Irish traditional music. I just didn't know how it was all going to come together, but there it all happened for me, in my late 20s. I just thought that this is great."*
>
> –Enya on the success of *Watermark*

folk band, Clannad, playing keyboards and singing backing vocals. Enya left the band in 1982 to become a solo artist in partnership with Nicky Ryan, whom she met—along with his wife Roma, a lyricist—when he was Clannad's sound engineer.

Enya released her debut album in 1987, later put out as *The Celts*. Her 1991 album, *Shepherd Moons*, was a commercial success, spending 238 weeks on the Billboard 200 charts and selling 13 million copies worldwide. In 2000, "Only Time," the lead single off her fifth studio album, *A Day Without Rain*, reached No. 1 in Canada, Germany, Poland, and Switzerland. It was No. 2 in Austria, and became her only Top 10 single as a solo artist in the United States, where it peaked at No. 10 on the Billboard Hot 100. The record sold an estimated 16 million copies worldwide.

Enya is Ireland's best-selling solo artist, having sold 26.5 million certified albums in the United States, and an estimated 80 million records worldwide. Without doubt, she is one of the most successful music artists ever.

How to Play It

Watermark is the second studio album by Enya, released on September 19, 1988. It peaked at No. 5 on the U.K. Albums Chart and No. 25 on the Billboard 200 in the United States. In New Zealand and Switzerland, it reached No. 1, and has sold more than four million copies across the United Kingdom and the United States.

"On Your Shore" features a simple, beautiful solo that is best described as "dreamy." Play with a soft tone and think classical clarinet; play very lightly. Measure 8 has big note bend on the A♯. Watch the key signature, too.

Vital Stats

Clarinet player: Neil Buckley

Song: "On Your Shore"

Album: *Watermark*

Age at time of recording: 51

Clarinet used: unknown

Mouthpiece: unknown

Music by Enya
Words by Nicky Ryan

Kathy Jensen

Only Prince can have a funk song that features an equally funky clarinet solo!

Kathy Mendenhall Jensen was born in Minneapolis, Minnesota. She graduated from the University of Minnesota with a degree in music education, and did performance studies at Berklee College of Music. Her teachers include Brian Grivna, Jerry Bergonzi, and Mark Henderson.

Being proficient on all the woodwinds has allowed her to play in many pit orchestras for musical shows and theatrical productions—at the Ordway Center, Orchestra Hall, Guthrie Theater, and several performing arts venues in the Twin Cities. Minneapolis performances include local jazz venues such as the Dakota bar, The Artist's Quarter, and the Fine Line. As a member of the Hornheads, Kathy has performed with Prince and the New Power Generation on several international tours—concerts in Japan, Australia, and countries throughout Europe—as well as in the United States.

Jensen made nine recordings with Prince, two that became gold albums. The Hornheads have created two solo discs and have worked with many pop artists, such as Chaka Khan, James Brown, Phil Upchurch, BabyFace, Pedro Abrunhosa, Jimmy Jam, and Terry Lewis.

Kathy is now retired and living in Arizona with her husband, a professional trumpet player.

Kathy Jensen

"I remember Prince asking me, after a long day of recording, if I played clarinet. I said yes but didn't have it with me. He asked if I could go home and get it. So, after a couple more hours we began recording."

–Kathy Jensen

Prince

Rogers Nelson was born to two musician parents on June 7, 1958 in Minneapolis, Minnesota. He taught himself to play guitar, piano, and drums at an early age. Forming his first band in high school, he later signed with Warner Bros. in 1978. His first album, *For You*, gained only modest attention. But his second album, *Prince*, had the hit single "I Wanna Be Your Lover," which reached No. 11 on the pop charts. His first huge success came with 1984's *Purple Rain*, which served as the soundtrack to the film of the same name. It grossed $70 million at the U.S. box office, and earned him an Academy Award for Best Original Song Score. The soundtrack sold more than 13 million copies in the United States alone.

A seven-time Grammy winner, Prince scored Top 10 hits like "Little Red Corvette," "Purple Rain," "The Most Beautiful Girl in the World," No. 1 hits with "When Doves Cry," "Let's Go Crazy," "Kiss," "Batdance," "Cream," and successful albums like *Purple Rain, 1999*, and *Sign o' the Times*. He released 39 studio albums, and sold more than 100 million records. Prince was inducted into the Rock & Roll Hall of Fame in 2004.

Prince died from an accidental prescription drug overdose on April 21, 2016.

How to Play It

Come was Prince's 15th studio album, released on August 16, 1994. It was the final album under his name, due to problems with Warner Bros., his record label. For the remainder of his contract with the company, his name was represented by the "Love Symbol;" he was referred to as "The Artist Formerly Known as Prince."

"Come" is the lead-off track on the album, showing the sort of typical funk that only Prince could provide. The 11-minute track features some heavy-form parts, spotlighting solos from trumpet and trombone, then finally some wailing clarinet!

Since it's a heavy funk-style tune, forget that classical trained setup! Just play open and loud!

The solo has a lot of note bends and aggressive articulations. Notice how the major 3rd on the minor chord adds a pleasing dissonance throughout. Measures 9-12 have a great call-and-response with the backing horns. Measures 15 and 20 add the major 7th to the minor 7th chord, giving some edgy dissonance.

Vital Stats

Clarinet player: Kathy Jensen

Song: "Come"

Album: *Come*

Age at time of recording: mid-30s

Clarinet used: Buffet

Mouthpiece: Vandoren

Words and Music by Prince